PR~~AYERS~~
For The Hurting,
The Hopeful
and The Praiseful

Robert Sexton

Lulu.com Publisher

PRAYERS For The Hurting, The Hopeful and The Praiseful
© 2013 by Robert Sexton

New Edition (Original Edition Published in 2008)

ISBN- 978-1-300-86387-8

Published by Lulu.com

Printed in the United States of America

Italics used in quotations from Scripture
have been inserted by author.

Prayers for all of us
on the road of healing, change and victory.

Dedication

I dedicate this book to my father, William Sexton, Jr. who went to his heavenly home in 1952, when I was fourteen years old. I have missed you dad, but I look forward to seeing you again when it is my time to leave this temporary residence, when this first chapter of my eternal life has come to a close.

I know that those of us who remain here now (brother Bill, sister Carol, sister Ina and myself) look forward to the joyous reunion that we will have with you, mom and sister June – a reunion so wondrous it can only be made in heaven.

Introduction

These prayers, with the exception of one, were written during my morning devotional times over the period of a year. While they reflect, to some degree, my own knowledge and experience of the Lord, the meaning, depth and flow of each of them came from the inspiration of the Holy Spirit. It is my prayer that He will use them to lift up the hurting, the hopeful and the praiseful, to draw each of us closer to the Lord of all compassion, forgiveness, mercy and love.

We are all hurting, hopeful and praiseful children of the King. We are all of these things, in varying degrees, during the differing seasons and circumstances of our lives. Who among us, whether new or mature in the Lord, can say that we do not hurt at times, that our hope does not vary in intensity as the war wages between the flesh and the Spirit, that our praise does not flow as joyful shouts, then as gentle whispers. No matter the season, the circumstances, or the distance we have traveled in our Christian walk, no hurt can overwhelm us, the flame of hope can never be extinguished, and praise will ever be on our lips, for we are children of the King.

Acknowledgements

I thank you, Holy Spirit, my Counselor, Comforter and Strength, for the blessing of inspiration, for guiding my spirit, heart and hand in this labor of love. Without You I can do no good and lasting thing.

I wish to extend my gratitude to each person who reviewed various portions of the draft and provided corrections, improvements and encouragement.

I offer many thanks to my friend Pastor Dick Evans, who provided invaluable guidance and assistance during my navigation through the technical aspects of the word processing and book publishing worlds. Thank you, Dick, for your friendship, for sharing your expertise and patience, and for your encouragement. Thank you Dianne, for your encouragement and great suggestions on formatting.

Opening Prayer

How Can I Not Praise You ?

O Lord, my God, how can I not praise you,
  you who lifted me from the pit of darkness and death,
    lifted me to the Light of true life and eternal hope?
How can I not praise you,
  you who lifted the chains of my sin and cast them down
    between the shadow of a blood-stained cross
      and a sun-lit garden's empty tomb?
How can I not praise you,
  you, the author of all things great and small,
    the author of all things seen and unseen,
  for your compassion and mercy are boundless,
    your love unconditional and never-ending.
I praise you,
      for you are the author
        of forgiveness, freedom, and true joy.
    You inclined your ear to me,
      you heard the cry of my heart
        and turned my sorrow into dancing.
        How can I not praise you?
                Amen.

Table of Contents

"I cried out to him with my mouth;
his praise was on my tongue.
If I had cherished sin in my heart,
the Lord would not have listened;
but God has surely listened
and heard my voice in prayer.
Praise be to God,
who has not rejected my prayer
or withheld his love from me!"
Psalm 66:17-20

A Cloth Of Many Colors

My Father in heaven, hallowed be your name.
Your kingdom come, your will be done, on earth as it is in heaven.
  Thank you Lord for your Word,
    for the many promises you have made,
      for new beginnings.
  Yesterday is never lost or thrown away,
    all yesterdays have become the fabric of my testimony.
  Your hand, O Lord, has been upon the weaver's rod.
   You have used the threads
    of sorrow and joy,
      disappointment and victory,
      rebellion and repentance,
      despair and hope,
    and woven them into a thing of beauty,
     a precious cloth of many colors,
       crafted with love and adorned with grace,
        a living work in the weaver's hand,
          unique and useful for your purposes and your
          glory.
I thank you my Father, for your hand is upon me,
  you continue the work that you have begun.
  Let this cloth of many colors glorify you
    and bring others to the saving hand of the weaver.
         Amen.

"I thank my God every time I remember you. In all my prayers for all or you, I always pray with joy because of your partnership in the gospel from the first day until now, being confident of this, that he who began a good work in you will carry it on to completion until the day of Christ Jesus." Philippians 1:3-6

A Garden For Each Of Us

My Father in heaven, hallowed be your name.
Your kingdom come, your will be done, on earth as it is in heaven.
Thank you for this day Father, a day like no other,
a day of great beauty,
of blue skies,
leaves of green
and lush grasses of springtime.
You have made a garden for each of us to enjoy,
a place of blessing,
a place of peace and new beginnings.
In this garden we can see more clearly,
listen more intently,
and walk quietly with the Master.
Remind us Father, to come to this place
in the dew of morning and the cool of evening
to seek His company,
to feel His presence,
to hear His words of life.
Open the eyes of our hearts and the ears of our spirits
that we may know Him more fully in this place.
Almighty and loving God, create in me a longing for this garden,
this place of refreshing and assurance,
of joyous, thankful tears,
of desperation's cry and sorrow's unburdening.
Place in me a thirst for the waters of grace that flow from you,
to walk with heart-felt repentance,
to reach out in your love, with your hand,
to the lost,
the broken,
the oppressed,
and those without hope.

Remind me always, that without Jesus and the power of the Spirit
  I can do no good and lasting thing.
Remind me as I go into this day that you are with me always,
  and when I am with you in heart, mind and spirit,
    I am walking on holy ground.
              Amen.

"Because of the Lord's great love we are not consumed,
  for his compassions never fail. They are new every morning;
    great is your faithfulness.
I say to myself, 'The Lord is my portion;
  therefore I will wait for him.'
The Lord is good to those whose hope is in him,
  to the one who seeks him.
It is good to wait quietly for the salvation o f the Lord."
              Lamentations 3:23-26

Blessed

Blessed are those who seek after righteousness,
   for they shall find peace on the lighted path.
Blessed are those who praise the name of Jesus,
   for they shall know great joy.
Blessed are those who humble themselves before God and man,
   for they shall be lifted up.
Blessed are those who see Jesus in every face,
   for they shall see through the eyes of God.
Blessed are those who share their riches with the poor,
   for their treasures will be great in heaven.
Blessed are those who embrace the lonely and forgotten,
   for their hearts will be filled to overflowing.
Blessed are those who reach out to the wounded and oppressed,
   for they shall rise up on wings of victory.
Blessed are those who earnestly pray for selflessness,
   for they shall draw closer to the heart of God.
Blessed are those who love the unlovely,
   for they shall receive amazing grace.
Blessed are those who are persecuted for His name's sake,
   for they shall receive crowns in glory.
Blessed are those who walk in obedience and repentance,
   for they shall live in the fullness of the Spirit.
Blessed are those who call upon the name of the Lord,
   for theirs is the gift of eternal life.
                Amen.

"As the scripture says, 'Anyone who trusts in him will never be put to shame.' For there is no difference between Jew and Gentile—the same Lord is Lord of all and richly blesses all who call on him, for, 'Everyone who calls on the Lord will be saved.'
How, then, can they call on the one they have not believed in? And how can they believe in the one of whom they have not heard? And how can they hear without someone preaching to them? And how can they preach unless they are sent? As it is written ' Beautiful are the feet of those who bring good news.'" Romans 10:11-15

Blessed Be The Lord

My Father in heaven, hallowed be your name.
The heavenly choir sings praises to your name.
  "Blessed be the Lord,
    who was, and is, and forever shall be.
      Blessed be the Lord."
Blessed be the Lord who is above all things,
  who created all things and knows all things.
Blessed be the Lord whose love is never ending,
  whose compassion is without bounds.
Blessed be the Lord who hears the cry of his children,
  who answers "Here am I."
Blessed be the Lord who sees the motives of men's hearts,
  who separates good from evil.
Blessed be the Lord who reaches down
  to lift up the broken and abandoned.
Blessed be the Lord whose forgiveness
  is beyond the mind of man.
Blessed be the Lord who says
  "Come, leave the ways of man and follow me."
Blessed be the Lord who is no respecter of persons,
  who exalts the humble and brings down the prideful.
Blessed be the Lord who desires that no one should perish,
  who loves the sinner and hates the sin.
Blessed be the Lord who gives hope to the hopeless,
  a lighted path for the lost.
Blessed be the Lord, the Father, Son and Holy Spirit.
Blessed be the Lord, the one, the only true God.
  And the heavenly host sings:
  "Blessed be the Lord,
    who was, and is, and ever shall be.
      Blessed be the Lord."
                              Amen.

> *"Because your love is better than life, my lips will glorify you.*
> *I will praise you as long as I live,*
>   *and in your name I will lift up my hands.*
> *My soul will be satisfied as with the richest of foods;*
>   *with singing lips my mouth will praise you.*
> *On my bed I remember you;*
>   *I think of you through the watches of the night.*
> *Because you are my help, I sing in the shadow of your wings.*
> *My soul clings to you; your right hand upholds me."*
>   Psalm 63:3-8

Change Me And Mold Me

My Father in heaven hallowed be your name.
Your kingdom come, your will be done, on earth as it is in heaven.
  You created all things, know all things, and see all things.
  You see all the stars in the firmament,
    yet in your compassion you see the child who falls.
  You know all that is of the earth and beyond,
    past, present and future,
      yet you know my words before they pass
        through my lips.
  Your word is the fountain of life,
    and your thoughts are wonderful -
      and so much higher than mine.
  Take my life, O Lord, and change me,
    mold me into a vessel that can be used mightily
      for your kingdom.
    Fulfill your purposes in and through me,
      to reach the lost, the abandoned, the sick,
        the hurting, and those without hope.
    Without you life has no true meaning,
    With you there is joy, peace and hope eternal.
I love you my Father,
                Savior, Lord and Friend,
                Counselor, Comforter and Strength.
You are the author of all love and compassion.
  Expand in me your love and compassion
    for all who are placed in my path.
                Amen.

> *"Because of the Lord's great love we are not consumed,*
> *for his compassions never fail.*
> *They are new every morning; great is your faithfulness."*
> *Lamentations 3:22-23*

Confession, Contrition And Cry For Change

My Father in heaven, hallowed be your name.
Your kingdom come, your will be done, on earth as it is in heaven.
   In that day love will replace hatred, selfishness and indifference.
      Evil will be no more.
Father, I cry out to you in the blessed name of Jesus
   to open my heart to all the love you have for me,
     that I may love others as you do -
     unconditionally and completely.
   Without love I am nothing, an empty drum,
     a river bed without rain.
Lord, I confess that I am, and have been,
   full of myself, my plans, my activities and my desires.
   I have not sought your face in all things,
     my will has been placed before your will.
   I have not lived sacrificially as Jesus has commanded.
Change my heart, O Lord, mold me into the servant
   that you want me to be.
   Help me to think more highly of others
     than I do of myself.
   Help me to put others first and to count sacrifice as a blessing.
   Give me a contrite heart
     with the desire and strength to do your will.
I confess that my relationship with you has been very shallow.
   I have not loved you with all my heart, mind, will and strength.
   Help me to receive your love –
     how can I give that which I have not been able to receive?
   My praise for you has been seldom and without passion,
     the joy of my salvation inconsistent and weak.
   Heal me and change me lest I go down to the grave
     brokenhearted and in shame.
   I know that you love me, my Father, Savior, Friend and Comforter.
     You have reminded me of that many times in many ways.
   I ask that you move that knowledge from my head to my heart.
Forgive me Lord, for I have sinned against you
   and against those around me.

Let no vestige of unforgiveness, selfishness or pride
  remain in my heart, that I may be right with you.
You have a plan and purpose for my life.
  Give me wisdom, patience and understanding
    for the road ahead.
I thank you and praise you, O Lord, for you have heard me,
  and your hand is upon me.

Amen.

*"I love the Lord, for he heard my voice; he heard my cry for mercy.
Because he turned his ear to me, I will call on him
  as long as I live."*

Psalm 116:1-2

Convict, Discipline And Restore Me

My Father in heaven, hallowed be your name.
Jesus, you are the King,
  the King over all who see heaven's light.
  You came to bring light to the darkness,
    freedom to the captives, life to the dead.
  I was dead in my sins and you forgave me,
    removed the chains of my guilt and gave me life.
  Today I walk in victory because of you.
  Today I have a hope, a purpose,
    and life more abundantly.
  Heal the wounds of my past and anoint me with the Spirit
    to lead others to you,
      to heal the wounded and rescue the lost in your name.
  Let me proclaim your name to all who can hear.
  Let me live according to your precepts, O Lord,
    let obedience be the way of my journey.
  Do not abandon me to the ways of the flesh;
    convict, discipline, and restore me.
  Let me be a vessel of your love, a purveyor of your truths,
    girded in the power and grace of your Word.
  I am a sinner saved only by your grace.
    Today is a joy, tomorrow is a hope.
  I praise you, for your love and compassion
    are beyond my understanding, beyond what I can hold.
  Open my heart that I may receive your love to the full.
    How can a man give what he has not received?
  Open my heart that I may receive and give
    love unconditional, love without bounds.
  Let this love heal wounds, restore the broken,
    bring peace where there is agony,
      and shine light upon the ways of your truth.
  I am the servant, you are the Master.
  Your loving hand is upon me even unto the end of the age.

I love and praise you my Father,
                  Savior, Lord and Friend,
                  Counselor, Comforter and Strength.
      Go before me today and always.
             Amen.

"My son, do not despise the Lord's discipline and do not resent his rebuke, for the Lord disciplines those he loves, as a father the son he delights in."
Proverbs 3:11-12

"Let love and faithfulness never leave you; bind them around your neck,, write them on the tablet of your heart.
Then you will win favor and a good name in the sight of God and man."
Proverbs 3:3-4

Courage, Peace, And Love For Others

Our Father in heaven, hallowed be your name.
You, who created all things large and small,
  all things seen and unseen,
    incline your ear to us.
    Hear the yearnings of our heart -
      to draw closer to you,
      to replace the old man with the new,
      to walk the path that you designed
        for each of us before the beginning of time.
You see all things, know all things and control all things.
  Though the demons howl and dart about in fury,
    your hand of protection is upon us.
  Our days were pre-ordained in your book of life.
  What man, what weapon, what disaster
    shall we fear?
  We praise and thank you
    for the moments of eternity
      that you have given to us in this place.
  The time here is a precious gift.
    Let us live it through you and for you -
      in humble servanthood,
        with a heart of gratitude and a song of praise.
    Help us each day, each hour, to seek your will,
      to hear your counsel and to do what you command.
    Give us courage in times of battle,
      peace when there is chaos,
        and love for the oppressed, the abandoned,
          and the lost.
We approach your throne of grace
  in the precious name of Jesus.
                    Amen.

"The Lord is with me; I will not be afraid. What can man do to me?
The Lord is with me; he is my helper. I will look in triumph on my enemies."
> *Psalm 118:6-7*

"But blessed is the man who trusts in the Lord, whose confidence is in him.
He will be like a tree planted by the water that sends out its roots by the stream."
> *Jeremiah 17:7-8*

Cry Of The Heart

My Father in heaven, hallowed be your name.
Your kingdom come, your will be done, on earth as it is in heaven.
  Father, you hear the cry of my heart.
    There is no cry, no matter how deep or how muffled,
      that does not reach your ear of compassion.
  You hear the cry of the heart for the lost,
    the broken and those without hope.
  You see the wounded,
    even the fallen bird does not escape your notice.
    How much more valuable is the fallen man,
      the oppressed woman to you.
    They are precious in your sight,
      and your loving hand reaches down to lift them up,
        to give them hope,
          to heal their woundedness.
Your love is more beautiful than the stars above,
  more wonderful than a field of summer flowers.
    You gave your only son on that terrible tree
      that none should perish.
    Even the vilest sinner with dark-stained soul
      is not beyond redemption.
    Your Word says:
      "If you confess with your mouth, "Jesus is Lord",
      and believe in your heart that God raised Him from the
      dead, you will be saved. For it is with your heart that you
      believe and are justified, and it is with your mouth
      that you confess and are saved."
          Romans 10:9-10
Let the cry of my heart for others be a pervasive,
  even desperate thing, not diminished or overtaken
    by fleshly, worldly beckonings.
Change me and mold me into a good and faithful servant
  who seeks your will
    and extends your hand of mercy, compassion and healing
      to all who are placed in my path.
          Amen.

"Is not this the kind of fasting I have chosen:
to loose the chains of injustice and untie the cords of the yoke,
to set the oppressed free and break every yoke?
Is it not to share your food with the hungry
and to provide the poor wanderer with shelter—
when you see the naked, to clothe him,
and not to turn away from your own flesh and blood?
Then your light will break forth like the dawn,
and your healing will quickly appear;
then your righteousness will go before you,
and the glory of the Lord will be your rear guard..
Then you will call, and the Lord will answer;
you will cry for help, and he will say:
'Here am I'."   Isaiah 58:6-9.

Draw Me Close, O Lord

My Father in heaven, Creator of the universe,
  Creator of all that is seen and unseen,
   You see the hearts and know the thoughts of men.
    There is no thing that is hidden from you.
  I praise you in humility, with gratitude, O Lord,
    for you know me.
     You love me even when my thoughts are far from you
      and my heart is not right.
     You do not turn from me, a sinner saved by your grace,
      redeemed by the blood of Jesus the Messiah.
  I cry out to you in my pain and uncertainty and you hear.
    Your loving hand is upon me.
     You see through my mask,
      you know my brokenness.
    You draw me close when I am able and willing
     to enter into your embrace.
Tear down all walls of pride, hurt and self-will
  that keep me from the fullness of your embrace.
Help me to fathom the depths
  of your love, compassion and forgiveness
    that I may be healed, that I may be made whole.
Use me, in the power of the Spirit,
  as an instrument of your love, compassion and forgiveness,
    that many may come to know you.
I am wretched and weak,
  but I find goodness and strength and joy in you.
The angelic choir gives you resounding praise and worship.
  There is no silence in heaven's east and west,
    north and south.
  My soul longs to enter in to this wondrous exultation.
You are with me always my Father,
                Savior, Lord and Friend,
                Counselor, Comforter and Strength.
            I love You.
            Amen.

"Surely he took up our infirmities and carried our sorrows,
yet we considered him stricken by God,
  smitten by him, and afflicted..
But he was pierced for our transgressions,
  he was crushed for our iniquities;
The punishment that brought us peace was upon him,
  and by his wounds we are healed.
We all, like sheep, have gone astray,
  each of us has turned to his own way;
and the Lord has laid on him the iniquity of us all."
                    Isaiah 53:4-6

Draw Me Ever To The Cross

My Father in heaven, hallowed be your name.
Your kingdom come, your will be done, on earth as it is in heaven.
Thank you Father, for today, yesterday and tomorrow.
   Your hand is upon me and I rejoice in you.
Thank you for Jesus, my Savior, Lord and Friend,
   for true life, abundant life and the promise of a forever tomorrow.
Thank you, Holy Spirit, my Counselor, Comforter and Strength,
   for you shine light upon the Word,
      convict me of wrong attitudes, thoughts and actions,
         ease the pain of life's hurts and disappointments,
            lift me from the valley of weakness and fatigue,
               you gird me up with the power to run the race
                  that was planned for me from the beginning of time.
Lord God, who is like you,
   you who parted the waters,
      healed the sick and broken,
         raised the dead and forgave the vilest of sinners.
You are the same yesterday, today and forever.
   What fools we are when we turn away and follow other gods,
      gods wrought by men's minds and hands,
         gods who have no power to save, to heal and to change.
Draw me ever to the cross,
   salvation's hill and freedom's empty tomb.
Send me forth to tell of sweet mysteries to the lost,
   to lift up the broken with the Word,
      with your loving hand, forgiving heart.
   Let my personal testimony
      of your redeeming love and forgiveness
         be used for your glory,
            to minister to those without hope,
               to those who are searching and disheartened.
I praise you with all my heart, mind, soul and spirit,
   for there is light where there was darkness,
      peace where there was turmoil,
         true life where there was a striving after the wind.
               Amen.

> *"Let the name of the Lord be praised, both now and forevermore.*
> *From the rising of the sun to the place where it sets,*
>   *the name of the Lord is to be praised.*
> *The Lord is exalted over all the nations, his glory above*
>   *the heavens.*
> *Who is like the Lord our God, the One who sits enthroned on high,*
>   *who stoops down to look on the heaven and the earth?*
> *He raises the poor from the dust and lifts the needy*
>   *from the ash heap;*
> *he seats them with princes, with the princes of their people."*
>   *Psalm 113:4-8*

Each Day, Each Hour, Each Moment

My Father in heaven, hallowed be your name.
　You are the only true God,
　　the God of all compassion and mercy.
　Today is a day that you have wrought.
　　There is no hour, no moment
　　　that you did not ordain.
　Change me in this day,
　　draw me closer to the tree of love and sorrow
　　　on Calvary's Hill.
　　Dispel the darkness in the corners of my soul
　　　with your marvelous light.
　　Place me in full view of the empty tomb,
　　　and bless all who hear my victory cry.
　Let the meditations of my heart and the words of my mouth
　　be pleasing to you, O Lord,
　　　for you are deserving of all praise and honor.
　Pour your love through me
　　to the sick, the confused, the hurting and the lost.
　Open my eyes, my ears, my heart and my spirit
　　to those who need a touch from you.
　　　Bless them, heal them, lift them and save them,
　　　　for you are the God of all compassion and mercy.
　　　Even the fallen sparrow does not escape your notice.
　　　　How much more valuable is a fallen child to you.
　　We, your children, cry out to you
　　　and your ear is attentive to us.
　　　You see our tears and do not turn away.
　　　When sorrow turns to laughter you rejoice with us,
　　　　you dance with us in sun-lit summer fields.
　This day, each hour, each moment, was ordained by you,
　　and your love is so very welcomed,
　　　so eagerly embraced by each of us.
I praise you my Father,
　　　　　　Savior, Lord and Friend
　　　　　　Counselor, Comforter and Strength.

I thank you Lord, for the precious gift
of this day, this hour, this moment with you.
Amen.

*"This is the day the Lord has made ,let us rejoice
and be glad in it."*
                              Psalm 118:24

Far Beyond The Tumultuous Sphere

Father, hallowed be your name.
You are my heavenly Father indeed.
  You are not a distant, harsh and angry God
    who punishes and does not forgive.
  You do not abandon or ignore,
    you are with me always.
  Your loving hand is upon me,
    you speak words of encouragement,
      affirmation and affection.
  You hear me when I call, you answer in your time, in your way,
    you provide for all my needs.
  You know me better than I could ever know myself,
    your plan and purpose for my life is perfect,
      it is greater than my grandest dream.
  Your promises are always kept,
    you forgive me when I do not keep my own.
  When I am wrong you convict and discipline me,
    that I may learn and grow.
  You will continue to change me from day to day,
    glory to glory.
  Should the heavens fall I need not fear,
    your hand shall lift me far beyond this tumultuous sphere
      to a glorious, peaceful, happy place
        where there's no end to life and praise,
          just true servanthood and love in heaven's wondrous day.
  Thank you Father, for salvation's cross,
    the empty tomb, your only Son the sacrifice.
  Who is like you O Lord?
    Thank you for the Holy Spirit, the power to do your will.
    Let the lost hear your call,
      let them reach from evil's pit
      to grasp your waiting hand.
  I worship you, my Lord, my God.
    How can I not praise you?
                              Amen

"Because of the Lord's great love we are not consumed,
  for his compassions never fail.
They are new every morning; great is your faithfulness.
I say to myself, 'The Lord is my portion;
  therefore I will wait for him.'
The Lord is good to those whose hope is in him;
  to the one who seeks him;
it is good to wait quietly for the salvation of the Lord.
                    Lamentations 3:22-26

For Healing And Change

My Father in heaven, hallowed be your name.
   You are the only true God, the designer and maker of all things.
I praise you Lord, for you are the keeper of my soul,
   the light unto my path.
      I can do no good and lasting thing without you.
Search me, O God,
   show me what areas of my life must change,
      what secrets of my heart must be revealed and released,
         what wounds in my spirit must be embraced and healed.
You are my Father, you withhold no good thing from me.
   Your loving hand is upon me,
      your word is life,
         your promises are as cool springs
           in a dry and thirsty land.
Go before me into this day,
   lift me when I fall,
      be my courage when I am afraid,
         let the light of your love
         and the joy of my salvation
           shine in and through me
             to those who are placed in my path.
I praise you, O God,
         my Father,
            Savior, Lord and Friend,
            Comforter, Counselor and Strength.
I thank you, O God, for you are with me always -
   even unto the end of the age.
               Amen.

"O Lord my God, I called to you for help and you healed me.
O lord, you brought me up from the grave;
  you spared me from going down into the pit.
Sing to the Lord, you saints of his; praise his holy name.
For his anger lasts only a moment, but his favor lasts a lifetime;
weeping may remain for a night, but rejoicing
  comes in the morning."
                          Psalm 30:2-5

For Repentance, Change And Victory

My Father in heaven, hallowed be your name.
You are above all creation, all nature, all kingdoms, and all men.
Blessed is the nation that accepts you as their God,
   that honors you, obeys your commandments
     and embraces your Word.
May the leaders of this country seek You,
   and may we, its people, turn from our wicked ways.
You will not be mocked, and woe unto those who deny
   and mock you.
Touch the hearts of those who confess Christ but are far from Him.
Help me in my own walk with you,
   keep my tongue from slander or murmurings,
     deliver me from impatience, resentment or judgmentalism.
     Convict me of slothfulness or selfishness.
     Let me count the ways that you have blessed me and my family.
     Put a song of praise ever on my lips
       and let me extol your mercies and your love.
     Who am I but a passing shadow?
     Who am I that you should be mindful of me
       and have my name written in your book of eternal blessings?
     Who am I that you should die for me?
Wrap me in a garment of humility and praise.
   Take my hand this day and lead me on your path of victory.
I celebrate you, my Father, my Lord and my God.
Amen

> *"If my people, who are called by my name,*
> *will humble themselves and pray and seek my face*
> *and turn from their wicked ways, then I will hear from heaven*
> *and will forgive their sin and will heal their land."*
> *2 Chronicles 7:14*

For Strength And Resolve

Father in heaven, incline your ear to us.
  See through our fears and hear the cries of our hearts.
  Heal our brokenness and fill us with the power of the Spirit.
  Give us strength and a burning resolve
    to stay the course, to stay close to you,
      to find it joy to be persecuted for you.
  The voice of the martyrs cries out encouragement
    as they shout "Holy is the Lord, blessed is the Lord.
      Merciful and loving is the Lord of all hope,
        all redemption.
      Holy is the Lord, in Him we rest.
      Worthy is the lamb that was slain
        to receive honor, glory, and praise.
      To Him we raise our hands and voices and give thanks,
        for he will in no way lose those
          whom the Father has given unto him.
      We are his and he is ours, even unto the end of the age."
      Praise the Lord, praise the Lord.
Amen.

> *"Blessed are those whose strength is in you, who have set their hearts on pilgrimage.*
> *As they pass through the Valley of Baca, they make it a place of springs; the autumn rains also cover it with pools..*
> *They go from strength to strength, till each appears before God in Zion."*
>
> *Psalm 84:5-7*

Help Us To Be Strong In You

My Father in heaven, hallowed be your name.
Your kingdom come, your will be done, on earth as it is in heaven.
Hallowed be your name.
  It is a blessing, a relief O Lord,
    to know that you watch over the earth
      and you have ultimate control.
In these days there are wars and rumors of wars,
    hatred and discord,
      men have become lovers of themselves and do not honor you.
Some say that there is no God, others worship false gods.
False teachers preach a distorted gospel to tickle men's ears,
    where right is wrong and wrong is right,
      where whispers of doubt from the evil one
        are allowed to draw many from the lighted path.
Many would seek to destroy your people Israel,
    but you will not let your chosen people go down to the pit.
Woe unto those who persecute your people and defame your name.
Woe unto those who terrorize your people,
    who teach children hatred toward others
      and suicide as a way to kill and maim innocents.
Forgive them Father, for they know not what they do.
    You forgive all men when they repent
      and embrace Christ Jesus as their Lord and Savior.
    There is hope for the terrorist, hope for the terrorized,
      you desire that no one should perish.
    No man is without sin.
    No man is beyond redemption lest he blaspheme the Holy Spirit.
The battle is yours, O Lord.
    Help us to be strong in these last days.

"Finally, be strong in the Lord and in his mighty power.
    Put on the full armor of God so that you can take your stand
    against the devil's schemes.

For our struggle is not against flesh and blood,
but against the rulers, against the authorities,
against the powers of this dark world
and against the spiritual forces of evil
in the heavenly realms.
Therefore, put on the full armor of God,
so that when the day of evil comes,
you may be able to stand your ground,
and after you have done everything, to stand."
Ephesians 6:10-13

We praise you and our trust is in you, Almighty God,
Father, Son and Holy Spirit.

Amen.

"But now a righteousness from God, apart from the law,
has been made known, to which the law and the prophets testify.
This righteousness from God comes through faith in Jesus Christ
to all who believe. There is no difference, for all have sinned
and fall short of the glory of God, and are justified freely by his
grace through the redemption that came by Christ Jesus."
Romans 3:21-24

Here I Am Lord, Send Me

O Lord my God, help me today to move and act
   according to your precepts.
Let no unclean thing come out of my mouth.
   Let my yes be yes and my no be no.
Fill my mind with the beauty and wonder of your promises.
Today is all around me, tomorrow is a dream.
   Guide my feet upon the path that honors you today.
Let not the praises of men be my goal,
   let me seek to please you in humility and obedience.
   Help me to run the race toward the prize – the precious words
     "Well done my good and faithful servant".
Cleanse my heart and mind of all that is offensive to you,
   filling those emptied places
     with gratitude, love, and awe of you.
Tomorrow is a dream, let that dream be filled
   with hopes and plans to do your will, to honor you.
Strengthen and embolden me for the journey
    you have laid before me.
   Where confusion reigns let me bring wisdom and understanding.
   Where there is anger and strife let me bring peace.
   Where there is hatred and discord
    let me bring love and reconciliation.
   Where there is selfishness let me be selfless.
   Where there is unbelief let me believe.
Strengthen and embolden me for the journey
    you have laid before me.
You have called and I have answered
   "Here I am Lord. Send me".
                Amen.

"As the scripture says, 'Anyone who trusts in him will never be put to shame.' For there is no difference between Jew and Gentile – the same Lord is Lord of all and richly blesses all who call on him, for, 'Everyone who calls on the name of the Lord will be saved.' How, then, can they call on the one they have not believed in? And how can they believe in the one of whom they have not heard? And how can they hear without someone preaching to them? And how can they preach unless they are sent? As it is written, 'How beautiful are the feet of those who bring good news!'"
Romans 10:11-15

How Can I Praise and Thank You Enough?

My Father in heaven, hallowed be your name.
Your kingdom come, your will be done, on earth as it is in heaven.
  My Lord, who is like you?
    You lifted me from the pit of darkness and destruction
      and placed me on the lighted path,
        the path of peace that is Christ Jesus.
    When I cried out to you from the valley of emptiness
      and striving,
        when you saw me chasing after the wind,
          in your compassion you spoke to my heart and said
            "Be still my child, and know that I am God."
          You opened my eyes to the path of purpose and meaning
            that you had prepared for me before the beginning of time.
          I was dead in my transgressions and wounded in spirit,
            but your Word gives life,
              and there is healing in the precious name of Jesus.
  Who is like you Lord Jesus?
    for it is you who have said:
    "I am the way and the truth and the life.
    No one comes to the Father except through me." *(John 14:6)*
    You have started a work in me that you will continue
      until I am called to that home in glory.
  I beseech you, O Lord, to cast out all shadows
    of selfishness, pridefulness and doubt
      that cause me to stumble on the path of righteousness.
    Convict me when I am wrong and guide me
      in the ways of humility, repentance and forgiveness.
  You are God and I am not.
    I praise and thank you my Abba Father,
      Savior, Lord and Friend, Counselor, Comforter and Strength.
    Use me to share the good news with the lost,
      to lift up the oppressed and downtrodden,
        to reach out to the wounded and broken.

Your compassion is never ending,
   your love is beyond measure.
I receive your compassion and your love,
   let it be passed on to others in your name.
                    Amen.

"I cried out to him with my mouth; his praise was on my tongue.
If I had cherished sin in my heart,
*   the Lord would not have listened;*
but God has surely listened and heard my voice in prayer.
Praise be to God, who has not rejected my prayer
*   or withheld his love from me!"*
                    Psalm 66:17-20

"May God be gracious to us and bless us and make his face shine
*   upon us,*
That your ways may be known on earth, your salvation
*   among all nations."*
                    Psalm 67:1-2

How Long, O Lord ?

My Father in heaven, hallowed be your name.
  Help me, Father, to focus on you in this time of prayer.
  Let me lean on Jesus,
    remembering that his yoke is easy and his burden is light.
  I confess, O Lord, that my mind wanders
    to the events of yesterday,
      the cares of this day,
        and the concerns for tomorrow,
  Who is like you,
    you who has clothed me in the righteousness of Christ Jesus
      and in the power of the Holy Spirit.
    You have clothed me in righteousness and power,
      yet so often I go into the day with a covering of selfishness
      and in the weakness of the flesh.
  How long, O Lord, will I be disobedient to you?
    How long will my mind and heart wander
      to the things of this world,
        the things that lead to darkness, not to light?
    How long will I be deaf to the whispers of the Holy Spirit
      and blind to the way of selflessness, mercy and compassion?
    Lead me, O Lord, through the fires of repentance,
      that the dross of the flesh may be burned away
      and the precious gold of the heart of Jesus be revealed.
  Who is like you, O Lord,
    you who has the power over all
      yet hears the cry of the least of your children?
    Your thoughts are so much higher than mine.
      You see the road ahead.
        You know the beginning and the end.
    I place my trust in you and I praise you,
      for you will continue the work that you have begun in me.
    I praise you, for your patience is great
      and your compassion is never-ending.

You go with me into the day.
  You have lifted me higher
    and I rejoice in your presence and your promises.
                    Amen.

> *"Trust in the Lord with all your heart and lean not*
> * on your own understanding;*
> *in all your ways acknowledge him, and he will make your paths*
> * straight."*
>   *Proverbs 3:5-6*
>
> *"My son, do not despise the Lord's discipline and do not despise*
> * his rebuke,*
> *because the Lord disciplines those he loves, as a father the son*
> * he delights in."*
>   *Proverbs 3:11-12*

I Place My Trust In You

My Father in heaven, hallowed be your name.
  You are my Father indeed.
  You created me in my mother's womb.
  You knew my name even before I was conceived.
  From the beginning of time you had a plan and a purpose
    for my life.
  Your loving hand has been upon me,
    even when I was far from you and steeped in sin.
  Many times you rescued me from the pit.
    When I spoke your name in vain, in anger and rebellion,
      even then you did not abandon or condemn me.
  Your patience and love are beyond the minds of men.
  O Lord, you opened my eyes that I might see my depravity,
    my helplessness and need for you.
  I praise you and thank you,
    for you did not let me go down to the grave in shame.
    You lifted me up and gave me hope,
      hope in your everlasting love,
        your forgiveness and redemption,
      hope in the finished work on Calvary's hill.
    You gave me a Savior, I could not save myself.
    You restored me to true life,
      you rescued me from the domain of darkness,
        the clutches of the evil one.
  My Lord, my God, joy springs from the knowledge of these things,
    it is sustained by the Spirit that you have placed within,
      it grows in the Word that you plant in my heart.
  Convict me each day that I may not sin against you.
  Help me to love as you love, forgive as you forgive,
    let your hand of compassion reach through me to those in need.
  Let me not judge others, lest I be judged and found wanting.
    Who am I, O Lord, but a sinner rescued by your grace.
  Let praise be ever on my lips, gratitude ever in my heart.

You are my Father, I am your child.
You are my Savior, Lord and Friend,
  I am your servant humbled by your redemptive sacrifice
    and everlasting friendship.
You are my Counselor, Comforter and Strength,
  I am your temple, eager to listen, to change, and to act.
There is none like you, Almighty God,
  I place my trust in You.

Amen.

*"May the God of all hope fill you with all joy and peace
as you trust in him, so that you may overflow with hope
by the power of the Holy Spirit."*
Romans 15:13

In The Morning Of Salvation's Love

My Father in heaven, hallowed be your name.
Hallowed be your name, O Lord.
  I thank and praise you, for you provide for me and my family.
    You meet all of our needs.
  Your love and concern is wider, deeper and higher
    than I can perceive.
  You are holy.
  O Lord, there is no spot or blemish in you.
  The heavens and earth are full of your glory.
    Were I to sing of your mercies and the work of your hands
      the hours of the day could not contain my words.
  You are my loving Father, what can man do to me?
    Where there is hatred and discord
      let me be the bearer of your light.
    Where there is ignorance and unbelief
      let me proclaim your precious Word.
    Where there is fear and hopelessness
      let me reach out your hand of peace and hope.
  In the morning of salvation's love
    you lift up the wounded and the lost.
  During the precious day of sanctification's journey
    you convict, change and mold.
  In the evening of the traveler's stay
    you calm the weary and the faithful
      with whispers of heaven's call.
  The heavenly choir sings praises to your name
    and joy abounds at the gates when each saint enters in.
  You are worthy of all praises, honor and glory.
  Thank you Father, in the precious name of Jesus the Messiah.
                    Amen.

> *"He gives strength to the weary and increases the power of the weak.*
> *Even youths grow tired and weary, and young men stumble and fall;*
> *But those who hope in the Lord will renew their strength.*
> *They will soar on wings like eagles; they will run and not grow weary, they will walk and not be faint."*
> *Isaiah 40:29-31*

Increase My Joy Indeed

My Father in heaven, Father of my heart and soul,
  hallowed be your name.
You are the only God, there is no other.
Help me today to rise above all that is ugly, unseemly or hurtful.
Increase my joy and let it overflow to others.
Hold my hand Christ Jesus, and walk with me
  on today's smooth or rocky road,
    on the path you have ordained for me.
Forgive my trespasses as I forgive those who trespass against me.
Show me where unforgiveness lingers on in my heart
  and lift those painful, biting chains that they may be cast away.
Convict me that I may be obedient to you, O Master.
      There is such freedom in obedience,
        a release from bondage for the soul,
          a drawing close in truth to you.
You are the Master, I am the servant.
  Let me hold others as greater than myself,
    seeing through your eyes of truth and grace.
  Let me care for the oppressed, the lonely, the broken and forgotten,
    reaching out with your hand of compassion.
  Let me stand for truth, to honor all that is right and pure,
    to abhor all that is evil, cruel or selfish.
  Increase my joy indeed,
    that it may flow to others in abundance,
      lifting heads and giving hope.
  Draw me closer, expand my faith,
    let the testimony of my lips give praise to you.
I need you my Father, Savior, Lord and Friend.
  You have filled that empty place within,
    filled it with the Spirit of power and of grace.
  Your love is all I need,
    it is brighter than the moon, the stars, the sun.
  Behold your child.
    Receive my love, gratitude, and adoration.

You are my Father, I am your child.
  Hallowed be your name.

Amen.

> *"Come, let us sing for joy to the Lord;*
>   *let us shout aloud to the Rock of our salvation.*
> *Let us come before him with thanksgiving*
>   *and extol him with music and song.*
> *For the Lord is the great God, the great King above all gods.*
> *In his hand are the depths of the earth,*
>   *and the mountain peaks belong to him.*
> *The sea is his, for he made it, and his hands formed the dry land*
> *Come, let us bow down in worship,*
>   *let us kneel before the Lord our Maker;*
>   *for he is our God and we are the people of his pasture,*
>   *the flock under his care."*
>   *Psalm 95:1-7*

Instruments of Love, Forgiveness and Healing

Our Father in heaven, hallowed be your name.
  Your kingdom come, your will be done on earth as it is in heaven.
    ….and the lion will lie down with the lamb,
      sickness and sorrow will be no more,
      hatred, envy and malice will be unknown,
        and the day of evil will have come to a close.
Today we beseech you, O Lord,
  to touch our hearts and minds with your gentle hand,
    that we may be instruments of love, forgiveness and healing
      in the precious name of Jesus.
Convict us of all that is unworthy in our lives
  and give us the desire and strength to change.
Let us be as children at the feet of the Master,
  who hear, believe, and go forth with great joy and celebration.
Who among us is without need of the kindness and gentleness
  of the Shepherd's voice and hand?
Who can say "I have no need of redemption, restoration,
  hope and affection?"
Who among us can say "I am the great I Am?"
Let us go forth with a song of gladness,
  a testimony of praise for all you have done
    and all you will ever do,
  a testimony of answered prayer and transformation,
    a confession of ashes turned to beauty.
We love you, Lord,
  we thank you for lifting us out of darkness into the light.
          Amen.

> *"Praise be to the God and Father of our Lord Jesus Christ,*
> *the Father of compassion and the God of all comfort,*
> *who comforts us in all our troubles,*
> *so that we can comfort those in any trouble with the comfort*
> *we received from God."*
> *2 Corinthians 1:3-4*

It Is Good To Be Alive

My Father in heaven, hallowed be your name.
  Thank you for this day,
    for the peace and quiet of the morning,
      the gentle breezes,
        the melodious sounds of these little winged friends.
  It is so good to be alive.
  It is so good to be alive in you.
  It is so good to be alive knowing
    that you have a purpose and plan for my life.
  It is so good to be alive knowing
    that your hand of protection is upon me.
  It is so good to be alive knowing
    that you are changing me,
      in your time and in your way,
        to be more like the Master.
  It is so good to be alive knowing
    that you have chosen me as your beloved child,
      I am forgiven,
        and I will live in the house of the Lord forever.
  It is so good to be alive.
  Who is like you, O Lord?
    Not a star can fall from the sky
      or a hair fall from my head
        without your knowledge.
  You give life and give it more abundantly.
    You empty the jar filled with corrupted, broken and ugly things,
      and you fill it with pure, whole and beautiful things
        in your time and in your way.
  Who is like you, O Lord,
    you who has the power over all things,
      you who cares for a single child,
        you who gave the supreme sacrifice
          that none of us should perish.
  It is so good to be alive in you.
    Today is like no other.
      Every day with you is a new day.

I praise you and love you
    my Father,
        Savior, Lord and Friend,
            Counselor, Comforter and Strength.
                Amen.

"My heart is steadfast, O God; I will sing and make music
* with all my soul.*
Awake, harp and lyre! I will awaken the dawn.
I will praise you, O Lord, among the nations; I will sing of you
* among the peoples.*
For great is your love, higher than the heavens; your faithfulness
* reaches to the skies.*
Be exalted, O God, above the heavens, and let your glory
* be over all the earth."*
*   Psalm 108:1-5*

It Is You, Lord

My Father in heaven, hallowed be your name.
Your kingdom come, your will be done, on earth as it is in heaven.
  I praise you Lord, for your mercies are great
      and your compassion never ends.
        It is you who lifted me from the pit,
            closed the mouth of the lion.
        It is you who cast my sins into the sea of forgetfulness.
        It is you who set my feet upon a Rock,
            gave me a future and a hope.
        It is you who heard my anxious cry and placed your quiet,
            loving hand upon me.
        It is you who saw my tears and placed a warm, healing balm
            upon my woundedness.
        It is you who knew my fears, held me close
            and whispered sweet assurance.
        It is you who took me to your breast
            and spoke the words I'll ne'er forget:
            "You are mine my child,
                I'll love you in all seasons of this life and of the next."
        It is you who shatters the darkness of my soul
            with brilliant light.
        It is you who placed ne'er ending gratitude in my heart –
            a joyful song upon my lips.
  I praise you my Father,
                    Savior, Lord and Friend,
                    Counselor, Comforter and Strength.
  I praise you Lord, for your mercies are great
      and your compassion never ends.
                        Amen.

"Praise be to the Lord, for he showed his wonderful love to me
when I was in a besieged city.
In my alarm I said 'I am cut off from your sight!'
Yet you heard my cry for mercy when I called to you for help."
Psalm 31:21-22

Let Not The Seasons Pass Me By

My Father in heaven, hallowed be your name.
  Thank you for the sweet sounds of birds singing,
        for gentle summer breezes,
        for sunshine after the rain.
  Thank you for morning, noon and night,
    for summer, fall, winter and spring,
      for all seasons of life--
        each holds much meaning,
          each has its reason in your divine plan.
Lord God, let not the hours, days, weeks and months
  pass me by without notice.
Open the eyes of my heart and the ears of my spirit
  to all gifts in time and space.
    Let me hold the sounds of children playing as a joy,
      let me wonder in the unselfishness of many,
        let me see the face of Jesus
          in each man, each woman, each child,
            and let not their station, loveliness or homeliness
            cloud the image of the Master.
Let me go forth into this day
  with an attitude of humility and repentance.
    Cast out all pride and willfulness
    and mold me into the vessel that you have designed.
Thank you for the Way, the Truth and the Life
  that is Christ Jesus.
               Amen.

> *"You are the light of the world. A city on a hill cannot be hidden. Neither do people light a lamp and put it under a bowl. Instead they put it on its stand, and it gives light to everyone in the house. In the same way, let your light shine before men, that they may see your good deeds and praise your Father in heaven."*
> *Matthew 5:14-16*

Let The Flower Grow

My Father in heaven, hallowed be your name.
You are awesome in all ways that could be counted.
You see all the stars in the firmament.
You know all the peoples of the earth,
  you know the names of each of the six billion people.
You hear the prayers of the saints,
  and if all prayed at the same time,
    O Lord you would hear each one.
Your thoughts, your mind are so much higher than mine.
I am as a grain of sand upon the ocean's shore, but you know me,
  you loved me and had a plan for my life
    even while I was in my mother's womb.
You knew all the events of my life even before they occurred.
Your hand has been upon me even when I did not know it,
  even while I was steeped in my sin.
You delivered me from destruction,
  --not once, but many times that I am aware of,
    and many times that I have never known.
Search my heart this day, O Lord,
  and see if there is any darkness within.
Open my eyes that I may see all that is unlovely to you.
Convict me and change me,
  cast my pride, stubbornness and lust for things of this world
    into the abyss.
Let the flower of compassion, charity and unselfishness
  blossom within me,
    that the world may see the face, the heart and the hand
    of Christ Jesus.
There is no greater love, O Lord,
  than that which you have showered upon me.
  Let the flower grow.
I love you, O God,
  my Father,
    Savior, Lord and Friend,
    Counselor, Comforter and Strength.
     Let the flower grow.
             Amen.

"The Lord is my rock, my fortress and my deliverer;
my God is my rock, in whom I take refuge.
He is my shield and the horn of my salvation, my stronghold."
Psalm 18:2

Let The Rain Fall

Let the rain fall, let the rain fall,
There's no power without you, let the rain fall.

Lift up the broken, heal the infirmed,
Give hope to the hopeless, joy in the morn.
Wash away pride, break the yoke of denial,
Cleanse us from guilt, and help us forgive.

Let the rain fall, let the rain fall,
There's no power without you, let the rain fall.

Cast out the darkness, let the light shine,
Fill the soul's emptiness with the divine.
Your call to the altar let no one deny,
With praise, adoration, to lift your name high.

Let the rain fall, let the rain fall,
There's no power without you, let the rain fall.
                              Amen.

> *"Therefore I glory in Christ Jesus in my service to God.*
> *I will not venture to speak of anything except what Christ*
> *has accomplished through me in leading the Gentiles to obey God*
> *in what I have said and done – by the power of signs*
> *and miracles, through the power of the Spirit.*
> *So from Jerusalem all the way around to Illyicum, I have fully*
> *proclaimed the gospel of Christ."*
>
> *Romans 15:17-19*

Let Today Be Lived For You

My Father in heaven, hallowed be your name.
Your kingdom come, your will be done, on earth as it is in heaven.
Watch over me today, O Father, and direct my steps
   that I may not wander from the lighted path.
Convict me through the power of the Spirit
   that my eyes may not sin against you
      by drifting to the right or to the left.
Change my heart, O God, and do not leave me as I am.
   Cast out all that is unlovely,
     all that is unworthy,
       all that would bring shame to my countenance
         should I stand before you this day.
I praise you, for you are a loving and patient Father.
   You teach, admonish and discipline,
     all of this you do with love.
   Your patience is deep and wide,
     you are slow to anger.
   Forgive my trespasses as I forgive those who trespass against me.
     Forgive my prideful thoughts and willful actions
       and help me to live a humble and a better way.
   Your patience, forgiveness and love are beyond
     my comprehension, beyond how I have lived each day.
   When I am down you lift me up,
     when I rejoice you celebrate with me.
   You do not abandon or reject,
     your strong right hand of love stays on and around me.
   I need not fear, what can man do to me,
     my name is written in your book,
       my eternal home is beyond the stars.
I love you, my Father,
   my Savior, Lord and Friend,
     my Counselor, Comforter and Strength.
   Let my joy and assurance be shared
     with all who are placed in my path.
   Let today be lived for you.
               Amen.

*"One of the teachers of the law came and heard them debating.
Noticing that Jesus had given them a good answer, he asked him,
'Of all the commandments, which is the most important?'
'The most important one,' answered Jesus, 'is this:
Hear, O Israel, the Lord our God, the Lord is one.
Love the Lord with all your heart and with all your soul
and with all your mind and with all your strength. The second
is this: Love your neighbor as yourself. There is no commandment
greater than these.'"*   *Mark 12:28-31*

Lift Up Dry Bones

My Father in heaven, hallowed be your name.
Lord God, who is like you?
  You created the firmament and everything in it,
    there is no star that you do not know.
  Who is man, that you should be mindful of him,
    yet you knew each of us from the beginning of time,
      you knit us together in our mothers' wombs.
  You love us with an unconditional and everlasting love.
  Your compassion is boundless,
    you know the condition of our hearts,
      you hear our praise, you hear our cries,
        there is nothing hidden from you.
Lord God, open the portals of heaven
  and pour out your healing grace upon your people.
Ignite a growing faith and boldness in each of us.
  You healed many through Jesus, in the power of the Spirit,
    and you are the same yesterday, today and forever.
Empower your church, bring it to life,
  and let it be used to bring many to you.
Open our eyes, Lord, to the chains that bind,
  to that which tethers us to lukewarmness.
Release us, change us.
Let the power of our testimonies and the praise from our lips
  be a healing balm for the wounded and discouraged.
Who is like you, O Lord, you who healed the lepers
  and raised the dead.
There is no thing that you can not do.
  Replace apathy with excitement,
    let the life-giving waters of the Holy Spirit
      flow over dry bones and lift them up
        as an eager army equipped for the battle for men's souls.
  You go before, behind and within us.
    Give us the strength to hold high the banner of Christ Jesus,
      the willingness to lay down all that we hold dear
        in this world,
          and the courage to engage in the battle.

Above all, dear Lord, let us love you
with all our hearts, minds, souls and strength
and let us love our neighbors as ourselves.

For it is written:

"If I give all I possess to the poor,
and surrender my body to the flames,
but have not love, I gain nothing."   1 Corinthians 13:3

Hear our prayer, O Lord.
Revive us this day,
bring greater joy to our hearts,
and let us bear marvelous fruit for you.
Amen

"Then he said to me, 'Prophesy to the breath; prophesy,
son of man and say to it, 'This is what the Sovereign Lord
says; .Come from the four winds, O breath, and breathe into
these slain, that they may live.'' So I prophesied as he
commanded me, and breath entered into them; they came to
life and stood up on their feet – a vast army."
Ezekiel 36:9-10

Loosed From The Bonds Of Heaviness

My Father in heaven, hallowed be your name.
  You reside over all the nations, over all worlds.
  There is no thing that you did not create.
  Woe unto those who deny you,
    their destiny in darkness is sealed
      unless they turn and embrace the Light.
  Woe unto those, O Lord, who have confessed Jesus
    as Lord and Savior,
    but have denied the power of their testimony,
      those who are ashamed of Jesus and his Word,
        for it is written:

> *"If anyone is ashamed of me and my words in this adulterous*
> *and sinful generation, the Son of Man will be ashamed of him*
> *when he comes in his Father's glory with the holy angels."*
> *Mark 8:38*

Lord God, you who has the power over all,
  embolden the timid through the power of the Spirit,
    bring words of hope through the lips of the faltering,
      lift joyful praise and honor
        from the hearts of the worshippers.
  How long, O Lord, will your people live with their heads bowed
  in quiet defeat?
    Lift them up, focus their eyes upon you,
      loose them from the bonds of heaviness
        that abound in this dark world.
    Give life to their testimony,
      eternal purpose to their days,
        and joy, power and freedom in you
          that can not be denied by the lost
          and those in need of hope.
Who is like you, O Lord,
  your compassion is boundless,
    your grace and forgiveness beyond understanding,
      your love is unconditional and pure.

Bless your servants with an extra measure of faith,
   trust and charity.
The days are short and many have not heard that Jesus saves.
     You are with us always,
        you go before and behind,
           your hand of love and protection is upon us.
We love you our Father,
              Savior, Lord and Friend,
              Counselor, Comforter and Strength.
                 Amen

"To the Jews who had believed him, Jesus said, 'If you hold to my teaching, you are really my disciples. Then you will know the truth, and the truth will set you free.'"
John 8:31-32

Lord, Awaken, Stir And Inspire

Jesus, our Redeemer, Lord and Friend,
  we praise you and adore you.
  We implore you Lord,
    send forth the Spirit to the churches;
      awaken those who slumber,
        stir those who rest,
          inspire those who live in shadows.
      Give life to the dead,
        hope to the hopeless,
          strength to the weary.
  Rain down your Spirit anew
    and awaken your body to the great commission,
      to the power of your love.
Let all who confess your name hear your call.
Let the Spirit win the battle with the flesh,
    let every knee bow and every tongue confess
      that you are Lord.
Break the chains that bind,
    soften the heart and loosen the tongue for praise.
Let tomorrow be a day that the enemy fears,
    a day when the saints rise up
      in the power and counsel of the Spirit,
    a day when the song of victory can not be muffled,
    a day when courage and sacrifice shine forth in the darkness.
Open the eyes of the blind that they may see you
    and the gift of life that awaits them.
Put a new song of joy and hope ever on our lips
    and let us be a living testimony of praise
      until we leave this place for home.
             Amen.

"He gives strength to the weary and increases the power
  of the weak.
Even youths grow tired and weary, and the young men stumble
  and fall;
but those whose hope is in the Lord will renew their strength.
They will soar on wings like eagles; they will run
  and not grow weary, they will walk and not be faint."
                    Isaiah 40:29-31

Lord, Light The Road Ahead

My Father in heaven, hallowed be your name.
  Your kingdom come, your will be done, on earth
    as it is in heaven.
  Hallowed be your name, O Lord.
    Who is like you?
    Who is holy, without spot or blemish?
  Lord, light the road ahead with the fire of the Spirit.
    Burn off the stagnant waters of apathy and unbelief,
      ignite our hearts with the fire of passion –
        for saving lost souls,
        for lifting up the oppressed and broken,
        for being living testimonies
          of your saving grace and compassion,
        for praising and worshipping you.
  Lord, light the road ahead with the fire of the Spirit.
    Emblazon the sanctuary with your awesome power,
      that each man, each woman, each child
        may know that he or she is standing
          on holy ground.
    Let the fire of conviction and repentance
      draw the saved and unsaved to the altar
        of cleansing and salvation.
  Lord God, who is like you?
    Emblazon the sanctuary with your power.
      Touch each heart and soul
        with the fire of holiness, repentance, and salvation.
    Let each saint go forth into the day
      with passion for the lost,
                          the oppressed,
                          and the broken.
    Let each saint go forth into the day
      as a living testimony, praising and worshipping you.
Almighty God, you whose love, compassion and power
  are beyond measure,
    light the road ahead.
                        Amen.

"Be joyful always; pray continually; give thanks in all circumstances, for this is God's will for you in Christ Jesus. Do not put out the Spirit's fire; do not treat prophesies with contempt. Test everything. Hold on to the good. Avoid every kind of evil.
Thessalonians 5:16-22

Lord, You Know My Needs

My Father in heaven, hallowed be your name.
  You are the most Holy One on high.
  You look upon all creation and every man's heart.
    Who can hide his thoughts from you?
    Who can do deeds of good or deeds of evil
      without your notice?
My Teach me, O Lord, to do your will,
  to set aside desires of the flesh,
    to follow the ways of the Spirit,
      to walk on the path of righteousness
        where trod the feet of the Master.
Embrace me, O Father, draw me close and fill me.
  You know my needs better than I,
    show me the truth, the height and depth of them.
  Incline your ear to my words, your heart to my heart,
    and meet these needs I pray.
      Grace, O Lord, grace is what I need.
      Mercy, O Lord, mercy is what I need.
      Forgiveness, O Lord, forgiveness is what I need.
      Love, O Lord, love is what I need.
      Healing, O Lord, healing is what I need.
Bless me, O Lord, and help me in the power of the Spirit,
  to be a vessel of grace, mercy, forgiveness,
    love and healing.
  Let this vessel be poured out in your name
    for all who are placed in my path.
My Father in heaven, most Holy One,
  I praise and thank you, for your hand is upon me,
    even unto the end of the age.
          Amen.

"Praise be to the Lord, for he has heard my cry for mercy.
The Lord is my strength and my shield;
* my heart trusts in him, and I am helped.*
My heart leaps for joy and I will give thanks to him in song."
                    Psalm 28:6-7

"And my God will meet all your needs according to his glorious
riches in Christ Jesus. To our God and Father be glory
forever and ever. Amen."
                    Philippians 4:19-20

Lost and Now Found

My Father in heaven, hallowed be your name.
  Your kingdom come, your will be done, on earth as it is in heaven.
  Thank you, Father, for today, for all my yesterdays
    and all my tomorrows.
  Thank you for the sunshine and the trees,
    for all nature and all other created things.
  I praise you and love you.
    You are with me always.
    You have set my feet on the path toward wholeness,
      on the way of humility and gratitude.
    Your work in me is marvelous,
      that which I perceive and that which is not yet known to me.
    May your will be done, O Lord, not mine,
      for I was not present when you created the universe,
        when you created your plan and purpose for my life.
    Go before me into this day and remind me hour by hour
      to seek your face in all things large and small.
      You are the potter, I am the clay.
        Mold me into the vessel that you can use for your purposes,
          for your glory.
  Thank you for the blessings of this life,
    for they have lifted me up on wings of hope and joy.
  Thank you for writing my name in your Lamb's Book of Life,
    for I was lost, and now am found.
  Thank you for family and friends,
    for the marvelous church family you have placed me in,
      for loving and godly pastors
        who embrace and teach all of your Word.
  Thank you for my trials and tribulations,
    for it is in these times that I have drawn closer to you.
    You have lifted me out of the pit of destruction
      and given me true life.
    You have used the testimony of my sin and brokenness,
      of your redemptive love, forgiveness and power,
        to touch the hearts of many in need.

Who is like you, O Lord,
   for you have the power over all creation
     but you care for one lost soul.
Today is a new day.
  I praise you my Father,
           Savior, Lord and Friend,
           Counselor, Comforter and Strength,
  for you are making all things new in your time.
     I love you.
          Amen.

"Praise the Lord.
Praise the Lord from the heavens, praise him in the heights above.
Praise him, all his angels, praise him, all his heavenly hosts.
Praise him, sun and moon, praise him all you shining stars.
Praise him, you highest heavens, and you waters above the skies.
Let them praise the name of the Lord,
  for he commanded and they were created.
He set them in place for ever and ever;
  he gave a decree that will never pass away."
         Psalm 148:1-6

Love Never Fails

My Father in heaven, hallowed be your name.
Your kingdom come, your will be done, on earth as it is in heaven.
  Father God, the Spirit has convicted me
    of selfishness, impatience, anger and resentment.
  I confess these things, O Lord, and ask your forgiveness.
    Love is not selfish.
      It is written:
        "Love is not rude, it is not self-seeking". 1Cor. 13:5
    Love is not impatient.
        "Love is patient, love is kind". 1Cor. 13:4
    Love is not angry and resentful.
        "Love is not easily angered, it keeps no record of wrongs.
        Love does not delight in evil, but rejoices with the truth.
        It always protects, always trusts, always hopes,
          always perseveres. Love never fails." 1Cor. 13:5-8
Lord God, change my sinful heart.
  Cast out all darkness and replace it with the light of your love.
  Let me love as you love, unselfishly and unconditionally.
    Let me never forget, in my going out and coming in,
      my rising up and lying down,
        the height and depth and width of your love for me
        as measured on Calvary's tree.
      "If I speak in the tongues of men and of angels,
        but have not love,
          I am a resounding gong or a clanging cymbal.
      If I have the gift of prophecy
        and can fathom all mysteries and all knowledge,
        and if I have a faith that can move mountains,
          but have not love,
          I am nothing." 1Cor. 13:1-3
Forgive me Father, for my many sins against you
  and against my neighbor.
      "And now these three remain:
      faith, hope and love.
        But the greatest of these is love." 1Cor. 13:13
          Amen.

*"Let love and faithfulness never leave you; bind them around
your neck,
write them on the tablet of your heart.
Then you will win favor and a good name in the sight of God
and man."* Proverbs 3:3-4

Minister, O Lord, To Those In Need

My Father in heaven, hallowed be your name.
  Your kingdom come, your will be done,
    on earth as it is in heaven.
  Thank you for today, O Lord, for your goodness,
    for the power and wisdom of the Holy Spirit
      to convict and to change me.
  Thank for the desire to do what is right,
    to be at peace with all others and to walk in your ways.
  Lord, light my path today,
    let me not look to the right or to the left,
      to seek the self-indulgences of man.
    Let me seek your face in all things great or small,
      to see and hear those in need of a touch from you,
      to reach out in the power of the Spirit
        to minister your grace.
I humbly beseech you, O Holy and most loving God:
  To the wounded, minister healing.
  To the discouraged, minister hope.
  To the mourning, minister peace.
  To the lonely, minister your presence.
  To the weak, minister your strength.
  To the wretched, minister revelation.
  To the lost, minister "The Way, the Truth, and the Life".
Holy and most loving God, who is like you,
  for where there is darkness you bring light,
      where there is sorrow you bring joy,
      where there is anger and selfishness
        you bring forgiveness and humility.
Were I to go into this day without you
  I would be drawn by the lust of the flesh,
          deceived by all that glitters,
            subject to the trap of the evil fowler.
May the Word that you have hidden in my heart
  be ever on my mind and may praise for you
    be ever on my lips.

.

You hear me when I call,
  lift me when I fall,
    in you there is no darkness at all.
Most gracious, loving and forgiving Master,
  I honor and praise you,
    for I was lost and now am found,
        was empty, now am filled,
        was imprisoned, now set free.
Who is like you my Father,
                    Savior, Lord and Friend,
                    Counselor, Comforter and Strength.
                    Amen.

"Sing to God, sing praises to his name,
  extol him who rides on the clouds – his name is the Lord–
  and rejoice before him.
A father to the fatherless, a defender of widows,
  is God in his holy dwelling.
God sets the lonely in families,
  he leads forth the prisoners with singing;
  but the rebellious live in a sun-scorched land."
                    Psalm 68:4-6

No Greater Word Than Yours

My Father in heaven, hallowed be your name.
  You are my Father indeed.
  You care for me in the morning light,
    in the business of the day,
      in the evening shadows.
  You are ever-present and you know my deepest needs,
    my joys and sorrows, dreams and anxious thoughts.
  There is no thing about me that you do not know,
    my past, present and future,
      my acts of obedience and love,
        my times of disobedience and selfishness.
  You have started a good work in me,
    and you have promised to continue the work
      that you have begun.
  You have a plan and purpose for my life,
    a plan for good and not for harm,
      a purpose for your glory.
  I thank you and praise you,
    for you have rescued me from the darkness
      and given me hope,
        hope that is beyond what my mind can hold.
    It is written:
      "No eye has seen, no ear has heard,
        no mind has conceived what God has prepared
          for those who love him." 1Cor. 2:9
    You have not left me in ignorance,
      your Holy Book teaches, instructs, encourages
        and heals.
        There is no greater word than your Word,
          no greater love letter than this.
  You, Lord, are in my mind and you are opening my heart
    to receive the depth of your love,
      the meaning of true compassion,
        and the desire to live in an attitude of repentance
        and gratitude.

I praise you, Father, for you have known and loved me
    from the beginning of time.
I thank you, Jesus, my Savior, Lord and Friend,
    for you bore my sins on Calvary's hill.
I embrace and thank you Holy Spirit,
    for your counsel, comfort and strength that sustain me.
My Lord, my God, all earthly gifts and treasures
  are as nothing when compared to your love, forgiveness,
    and presence.
You go before me into the day, you light my path.
"Surely goodness and love will follow me
  all the days of my life,
    and I will dwell in the house of the Lord forever."
    Psalm 23:6
            Amen.

"Your word is a lamp unto my feet and a light for my path."
"You are my refuge and my shield; I have put my hope
  in your word."   *Psalm 119:105,114*

Of Awe, Gratitude And Love

My Father in heaven, hallowed be your name.
You are far above all that is seen and unseen, yet you see all things.
There is nothing in all creation that is not the work of your hands -
   the wonder of childbirth,
     the innocence and beauty of a little child,
      the gifts and talents of every man, every woman.
I am in awe of you.
We, your children, are like grains of sand, yet you are mindful of us.
   You know our hearts and our struggles.
   You deliver us from the muck and mire of sin's cruel hold.
   You place us in a garden of sweet freedoms,
    of joy's light,
     of a forever tomorrow.
You embrace us in our loneliness,
   take our hand when we are afraid,
    light the path when we have lost our way.
You are the Master yet your loving hand is upon us,
   we are so very precious to you.
We love you.
   Let this love grow and blossom.
    Let it become a beauteous thing that sows seeds of hope
     into the hearts of the captives.
You are my Father,
        Savior, Lord and Strength.
   Were I to go into the day without you
    I could find no peace, no comfort,
     and my joy, as the mist of morning, would be burnt away.
I love you and my trust is ever in you.
          Amen.

> *"The Lord is gracious and compassionate, slow to anger*
> *and rich in love.*
> *The Lord is good to all; he has compassion on all he has made."*
> *Psalm 145:8-9*

Put On The Full Armor Of God

MY Father in heaven, hallowed be your name.
  You are awesome.
    Without you the sun would not shine,
      the cheerful sounds of morning
        would cease to drift through my window,
          a cold, final darkness would descend
            upon the land and heart.
    With you, O Lord, there is light, life and hope.
    I place my trust in you.
      Surely the evil of the day will not overcome me
        because you go before and behind.
    With you there is joy in the morning,
      and I go forth into the day with confidence,
        for your righteous right hand is upon me
          and your armor protects,
            for it is written:
              "Finally, be strong in the Lord and in his mighty power.
                Put on the full armor of God so that you can stand
                  against the devil's schemes.
                    For our struggle is not against flesh and blood,
                      but against the rulers, against the authorities,
                        against the powers of this dark world
                          and against the spiritual forces of evil
                            in the heavenly realms.
                Therefore put on the full armor of God,
                  so that when the day of evil comes,
                    you may be able to stand your ground,
                      and after you have done everything, to stand.
                Stand firm then, with the belt of truth buckled
                  around your waist,
                    with the breastplate of righteousness in place,
                      and your feet fitted with the readiness
                        that comes from the gospel of peace.
                In addition to all this, take up the shield of faith,
                  with which you can extinguish
                    all the flaming arrows of the evil one.

Take the helmet of salvation and sword of the Spirit,
which is the word of God.
And pray in the Spirit on all occasions
with all kinds of prayers and requests.
With this in mind, be alert and always keep on .praying
for all the saints."   *Ephesians 6:10-18*

Who is like you, O Lord?
You have the power to save, to protect, and to guide.
You have the power over all,
    you created all things and know all things.
As far as the east is from the west,
    that is how far your eyes can see and your hand can reach.
You are God of the universe, yet you care about this child.
You are Abba Father and I am in awe of you.
I worship and praise you my Father,
                    Savior, Lord and Friend,
                    Counselor, Comforter and Strength.
            In you I trust.
            Amen.

"You hem me in – behind and before; you have laid your hand
upon me.
Such knowledge is too wonderful for me, too lofty for me
to attain."
            Psalm 139:5-6

Standing Firm With The Armor Of God

My Father in heaven, hallowed be your name.
My Jesus, my Savior, Bright Morning Star,
  you are above the heavens,
    but your light shines all around me,
      piercing the darkness, filling emptiness with hope.
  Your Spirit enfolds me, is within me,
    dispelling fears with faith and trust.
  You go before me into the battles of the day.
  You have given me your armor
    that I may fight the good fight against the devil's schemes.
    "Let me stand firm,
      with the belt of truth buckled around my waist,
        with the breastplate of righteousness in place,
          with my feet fitted with the readiness
            that comes from the gospel of peace.
      In addition to all this,
        let me take up the shield of faith,
          with which you can extinguish
            all the flaming arrows of the evil one.
        Let me take the helmet of salvation
          and the sword of the Spirit, which is the word of God.
        Remind me to pray in the Spirit on all occasions
          with all kinds of prayers and requests.
      With this in mind, help me to be alert
        and always keep on praying
          for all of my brothers and sisters in you."
                    Ephesians 6:14-18 NIV paraphrased.
  O Lord, were I to go into battle
    in my own strength and will alone, I would surely fall,
      but, fitted with your armor,
        wielding the shield of faith and sword of the Spirit,
          the battle shall be won.
My Savior, Lord and Friend, let me not slumber
  as the battle rages on for the souls of men.

I praise and thank you,
 for it is through your shed blood and the empty tomb
  that the battle is already won.
I thank you, Jesus, Bright Morning Star,
 for it is you who brought light into my darkness,
  it is you who brings freedom to the captives.
Amen.

"My heart is steadfast, O God, my heart is steadfast;
 I will sing and make music.
Awake, my soul! Awake, harp and lyre! I will awaken the dawn.
I will praise you, O Lord, among the nations;
 I will sing of you among the peoples.
For great is your love, reaching to the heavens;
 your faithfulness reaches to the skies.
Be exalted, O God, above the heavens; let your glory be over
 all the earth."
Psalm 57:7-11

Thank You For Springtime

My Father in heaven, hallowed be your name.
Incline your ear to me that I may honor you.
   Thank you Lord, for the sky so blue,
     a blue so deep its end I cannot see.
   Thank you for the greens in all their hues,
     wondrous colors of new life that excite the day in me.
   Thank you for the flowering trees of pink and white,
     tall stately trees with buds announcing spring.
   Thank you for the migrating birds
     that busily flit from tree to tree
      sharing beautiful calls and songs with me.
Lord God Almighty, who is like you?
   The beauty of your creation
     is more than the eyes and mind of man can hold.
   I praise you Lord, for planting within me
     an appreciation of these simple things,
      these marvelous gifts from you.
   I see you in all nature,
     in all of it your love comes through –
      your love comes through and touches me,
       it brings me closer, opens me to knowing more of you.
Lead me into this day and let me honor you.
   Place someone in my path who needs a word, a touch from you.
I love you Father,
        Savior, Lord and Friend,
        Counselor, Comforter and Strength.
           Amen.

> *"God saw all that he had made, and it was very good.*
> *And there was evening, and there was morning – the sixth day."*
> Genesis 1:31

Thank You For Tomorrow

My Father in heaven, the heavens rejoice at the sound of your name.
  Who is like you, O Lord, you who can see all things
    from east to west, from north to south.
  The mind of man can not conceive of all that you are,
    all that you have created,
      yet you care about me.
      You know my waking thoughts, my fears and joys,
        my brokenness and victories.
      You have lifted me higher, blotted out my transgressions
        with the blood of Calvary's hill,
          filled me with hope and joy at the sight of an empty tomb.
Thank you for today and all that you have in store for me.
Thank you for tomorrow, a forever tomorrow with you.
  Life will go on and on, I need not know the form or place,
    I need not touch a risen man or gaze upon your heaven's streets
      before it's time for me -
      I trust the promises you've made.
  Yes, Lord, it's you I praise with all that is within.
Thank you for your love, it is so much more than I can hold.
          Amen.

> *"For God so loved the world that he gave his one and only Son, that whoever believes in him shall not perish but have eternal life. For God did not send his Son into the world to condemn the world, but to save the world through him."*
>
> *John 3:16-17*

The Hope Of A Forever Tomorrow

My Father in heaven, hallowed be your name.
  Thank you for this day,
    for my coming in and going out,
      my lying down and rising up.
  You go before me, of this I am sure.
  Your promises are like springs in the desert,
    like honey to my soul.
  Were I to count all of my yesterdays
    the sum of them would be as one day on your eternal calendar.
  I give you all that I have ever been,
    all the joy, all the sorrow;
    all the pain, all the laughter;
    all the doubts and all the hopes.
I give you all that I am and all that I shall ever become.
  My Lord, I know full well that without you I am nothing,
    without you all my tomorrows would be lived
      in shades of darkness.
    With you there is an abiding peace
      that comes from the knowledge of your constant presence,
        the hope of a forever tomorrow,
          a forever tomorrow in glory.
  You are worthy of all praise, honor and adoration,
    you are worthy of all love and affection.
  Let today be lived for you.
    Place your healing hands upon my wounds
      and let the pathway of today be filled with forgiveness,
        humility, gentleness and love.
    Let no acts of selfishness or willfulness
      stress the bond between us, O Father.
    Teach me to love as you love,
      to walk in the ways of Christ Jesus.
            Amen.

"Therefore we do not lose heart. Though outwardly we are wasting away, yet inwardly we are being renewed day by day. For our light and momentary troubles are achieving for us an eternal glory that far outweighs them all. So we fix our eyes not on what is seen, but on what is unseen. For what is seen is temporary, but what is unseen is eternal."   *2 Corinthians 4:16-18*

The Life, The Way And The Truth

My Father in heaven, hallowed be your name.
  Your name is above all names.
Jesus, your name is above all others, it is precious,
  without flaw, stain or tarnish.
    You are the Messiah, the Life, the Way and the Truth.
      No man goes before you without trust, without faith.
      You are no respecter of persons –
        neither wise, nor rich, nor accomplished
          can enter your courts without bended knee and humble heart.
    Your grace and forgiveness are never ending
      for those who are willing to receive them.
      What is man if he has no hope, no assurance?
        He is a tree that has no root,
          a boat that has no rudder,
            that is blown from hither to yon by life's storms,
              that in the end perishes without purpose.
Jesus, Redeemer and Friend, it is faith in your name
  that gives the tree root, the boat a rudder.
      The tree has life, grows and flourishes in your light,
        gives beauty, shelter and comfort to those in need.
      The boat sustains a course,
        holds promise of safe landing for all within,
          promises peace in a way given and a way sure.
    You are the truth, eternal truth, the solid rock.
      The truths of man, devised to serve the self and not the Master,
        are naught but shifting sands.
    Draw us closer to the cross that we may see more clearly.
    Place words of praise upon our lips,
      help us to grow, to flourish in your light,
        to stay the course you have designed,
          to give comfort to the tossed, the battered,
            the lost and those without hope.
    Release the joy of our salvation,
      let it be a quiet, soothing word or boisterous sound
        that finds a home in listening ears and open hearts.

We are your children,
  you are our Father,
        Savior, Lord and Friend,
        Counselor, Comforter and Strength.
    We love and adore you.
                Amen.

"Jesus answered, 'I am the way and the truth and the life. No one comes to the Father except through me. If you really knew me, you would know my Father as well. From now on, you do know him and have seen him.'"   *John 14:6-7*

Unconditional Love And Unmerited Grace

My Lord, my God, Father of heaven and earth,
  Redeemer of the lost and broken,
    I honor you.
  I praise your name and the works of your hands.
    Your Word is life,
      it brings hope in times of despair,
        light in times of darkness,
          a sure path for the lost and confused.
    You give life, hope, light and a sure path
      to those who will receive you.
    Without you, surely the darkness would overtake me -
      as the ship's hull, battered and broken by the storm,
        is engulfed by the deep.
  O Lord, I call out your name and you rescue me.
    Though the winds and waves are furious
      and they crash against me,
        your saving hand sustains me.
      In the morning of your time the sea is calmed
        and the joy of my deliverance is upon me.
    How can I be beyond the reach of your hand,
      the power of your love?
        Were I to be in the deepest valley, the darkest jungle,
          I need not fear, for you are with me.
I honor you, I praise and thank you
  for the unconditional love and unmerited grace
    that you have bestowed upon me.
Search my heart and heal my woundedness.
  Convict me of all that is unlovely in your sight,
      help me to change, to cast off all chains that bind,
        and I will give you the honor and the glory forever.
      You are my Father and I am your child.
        I love you.
      You are my Redeemer, Lord and Friend.
        I love you.
      You are my Counselor, Comforter and Strength.
        I love you.

Let me be a light, shining bright upon a hill,
a harbinger of good news,
a voice of hope in the wilderness.
Amen.

"For God, who said, 'Let light shine out of darkness,' made his light shine in our hearts to give us the light of the knowledge of the glory of God in the face of Christ.
But we have this treasure in jars of clay to show that this all-surpassing power is from God and not from us. We are hard-pressed from every side, but not crushed; perplexed, but not in despair; persecuted, but not abandoned; struck down, but not destroyed." 2 Corinthians 4:6-8

With You, My Jesus

My Father in heaven, hallowed be your name.
Your kingdom come, your will be done, on earth as it is in heaven.
The kingdom of heaven is at hand,
  let me live it out in the power of the Spirit,
    in humility and grace,
      in kindness and love.
  Work in me, heal and change me,
    leave no blot of darkness, no selfish cords that bind.
  Draw me to your feet, O Master,
    let the cleansing tears of sorrows held too long
      fall like gentle rain.
Jesus, you are my loving Savior, Lord and Friend.
  Without you hope would be a fleeting thing,
    joy not deep, not real at all,
      hurt piling upon hurt, ne'er forgiven, always draining.
  Without you the chains of sin, cruel and biting,
    are ne'er broken or released.
  Here, with you, my Jesus,
    hope sustains,
      joy is full, not shattered by life's circumstance,
        hurts are lessoned by forgiveness' healing balm.
  With you, my Savior, sin's chains no longer bind,
    and freedom, life and love are mine.
  With you, my greatest Friend, I walk and talk and praise,
    ne'er alone again, ne'er succumbing to the problems of the day.
  I love you, my Savior, Lord and Friend.
Amen.

"Love is patient, love is kind. It does not envy, it does not boast, it is not proud. It is not rude, it is not self-seeking, it is not easily angered, it keeps no record of wrongs. Love does not delight in evil, but rejoices with the truth. It always protects, always trusts, always hopes, always perseveres.
Love never fails. But where there are prophecies, they will cease; where there are tongues, they will be stilled; where there is knowledge, it will pass away."

1 Corinthians 13:4-8

You Are Abba Father

My Father in heaven, hallowed be your name.
  Thank you for today, O Lord.
  This day is a new beginning, a blank slate.
    Write your instructions, your directions on this slate
      for the hours to be lived and the paths to be taken
        on this journey.
  Your will be done, not mine.
  Let my thoughts, words and actions be pleasing to you.
  You are the light of the world.
    Let me walk in the light,
      not looking to the left or to the right,
      not straying from the lighted path
        into the alluring shadows of the flesh.
    You go before and behind,
      have your hand of protection upon me,
        and increase my faith, strength and resolve
          through the power of the Word and of the Spirit,
            that I may not fall.
    When I stumble, overcome by weakness of the flesh,
      lift up, forgive, heal and restore me
        to the way you have ordained.
Who is like you, O Lord,
  your patience is long,
  your compassion unending,
  your love and grace amazing.
You are Abba (daddy) Father.
  Your love for me is unconditional and eternal,
    it is demonstrated in more ways than I can count or see.
  I love you Abba Father,
            Jesus, my Savior, Lord and Friend,
            Holy Spirit, my Counselor, Comforter and Strength.
                Amen.

> *"For I am convinced that neither death nor life, neither angels nor demons, neither the present nor the future, nor any powers, neither height nor depth, nor anything else in all creation, will be able to separate us from the love of God that is in Christ Jesus our Lord."*   *Romans 8:38-39*

You Are Good, O Lord

My Father in heaven, hallowed be your name.
  You are good, O Lord.
    Thank you this day, for life itself.
    Thank you for this opportunity to love and to be loved.
    Thank you for this time to seek your face,
      to sit at the feet of Jesus.
    Thank you for the sunshine that warms the heart,
      for rain that blesses growing things.
  You are good, O Lord.
    Thank you for the sounds of children laughing,
      for innocence and trust.
    Thank you for the hand that helps the poor,
      lifts up the downtrodden.
    Thank you for your power that heals,
      that touches the sick and mends the broken.
    Thank you for your promises,
      promises of hope and victory.
  You are good, O Lord.
    Thank you for courage in the face of adversity,
      strength to stay the course.
    Thank you for conviction from the Holy Spirit,
      the willingness to change.
    Thank you for the saints,
      your local body that supports, sustains.
    Thank you for the cross,
      the blood-stained tree you grew for me.
  You are good, O Lord.
    Blessed be your name.
  You are good, O Lord.
    Praise and honor and glory are yours forever.
                Amen.

"Know that the Lord is God.
It is he who made us, and we are his; we are his people,
* the sheep of his pasture.*
Enter his gates with thanksgiving and his courts with praise;
* give thanks to him and praise his name.*
For the Lord is good and his love endures forever;
* his faithfulness continues through all generations."*
                    Psalm 100:3-5

You Are Holy

My Father in heaven, hallowed be your name.
Your kingdom come, your will be done, on earth as it is in heaven.
You are holy. You are holy. You are holy.
  In this world of violence, chaos and confusion you are holy.
  In this place where truth is ridiculed,
     where right is called wrong, and wrong, right,
        your Word is holy, blessed be your name.
  Your compassion is boundless,
     you call those who are filled with pride,
        self-will and arrogance to repentance.
     you forgive all who are willing to turn from their wicked ways,
     you desire that no one should perish,
     you love the vilest sinner.
        No one who is willing is beyond salvation, is without hope.
           All have sinned and you love all.
You are holy, blessed be your name.
  You lift up the oppressed,
     mend the broken,
        give hope to the hopeless.
  Your hand of healing and restoration is upon us,
     your promises are more precious than silver or gold,
     you bring light into the darkness,
     you send a river of peace to extinguish the anguish of our souls.
You are holy, blessed be your name.
  Blessed be the name of the Lord.
  Blessed be the name of Jesus,
     who is the Way, the Truth and the Life.
  Blessed be you, O Lord, for you are holy.
                    Amen.

"And I saw what looked like a sea of glass mixed with fire and, standing beside the sea, those who had been victorious over the beast and his image and over the number of his name. They held harps given them by God and sang the song of Moses the servant of God and the song of the Lamb:

'Great and marvelous are your deeds, Lord God Almighty.
Just and true are your ways, King of the ages.
Who will not fear you, O Lord, and bring glory to your name?
For you alone are holy.
All nations will come and worship before you,
for your righteous acts have been revealed.'"

Revelation 15:2-4

You Are My Father Indeed

My Father in heaven, hallowed be your name.
　You are my Father indeed.
　　You knew me from the beginning of time.
　　　You knit me together in my mother's womb,
　　　　your hand was upon me as I was born.
　　　　　When I cried in my crib in the darkness of the night
　　　　　　you were with me.
　　　　　When I took those tiny, faltering steps and fell,
　　　　　　you lifted me up.
　　　　　When I grew tall and knew true sorrow and heartache
　　　　　　you were with me.
　　　　　When I cried in my bed in the darkness of the night
　　　　　　you were with me.
　　　　　When I took those long, faltering steps and fell,
　　　　　　you lifted me up.
　　　　　When I was blinded by the sin of my selfishness
　　　　　　and rebellion,
　　　　　　when I was confused, lost and overcome
　　　　　　　by emptiness and shadows,
　　　　　　　　you drew me to the light,
　　　　　　　　you drew me to the light of Christ Jesus,
　　　　　　　　you turned my tears of sorrow into tears of joy,
　　　　　　　　you showed me the way of good, not of evil,
　　　　　　　　you placed me on the path of righteousness and praise,
　　　　　　　　you knew my beginning, you know my end,
　　　　　　　　　none of my days have been hidden from you.
　　　Your purpose and plan for me is written
　　　　in the book of life.
　　　You have changed my heart and opened my eyes
　　　　to the needs of the lonely,
　　　　　　　　　the oppressed,
　　　　　　　　　　the discouraged,
　　　　　　　　　　　and those without hope.
　　Continue the work you have started in me,
　　　that I may be a vessel overflowing
　　　　with your love, compassion and grace.

I praise you, Father, for you have saved me from myself.
You have lifted me from the domain of darkness
into the Light that Is Christ Jesus.
I praise you, for you are my Father indeed.
Amen.

"For you did not receive a spirit that makes you a slave again to fear, but you received the Spirit of sonship. And by him we cry 'Abba, Father.' The Spirit himself testifies with our spirit that we are God's children. Now if we are children, then we are heirs — heirs of God and co-heirs with Christ, if indeed we share in his sufferings in order that we may also share in his glory."
Romans 8:15-17

You Are With Me Always

Almighty God, creator of all things large and small,
  you are with me always.
    When I am in the valley of tears you are there weeping with me.
    When I am on the mountain top of joy
      you are there dancing with me.
    You turn my sorrow into singing,
      disappointment into hope,
        painful shadows into peaceful light.
    You know my thoughts from afar,
      the desires of my heart are not hidden from you.
  I praise you, O Lord, for you know me and you hear my cry,
    your hand of love and compassion is upon me.
  I praise you, O Lord, for your promises are like honey to my lips,
    like cool, clear water in a dry and thirsty land.
  I praise you, O Lord, for you are with me always,
    even unto the end of the age.

"Surely goodness and love will follow me all the days
of my life and I will dwell in the house of the Lord forever."
Psalm 23:6

Amen.

"Where can I go from your Spirit? Where can I flee from your
   presence?
If I go up to the heavens, you are there; if I make my bed in the
   depths, you are there.
If I rise on the wings of the dawn, if I settle on the far side
   of the sea, even there your hand will guide me, your right hand
      will hold me fast.
If I say, 'Surely the darkness will hide me and the light become
   night around me,' even the darkness will not be dark to you;
      the night will shine like the day, for darkness is as light
         to you."   *Psalm 139:7-12*

You Lifted Me Higher

Your kingdom come, your will be done, on earth as it is in heaven.
The day shall come when the prince of this world
  will be cast into the fiery lake,
    when evil, suffering and disease will be no more.
    "Therefore God exalted him to the highest place
      and gave him the name that is above every other name,
        that at the name of Jesus every knee should bow,
          in heaven and on earth and under the earth,
        and every tongue confess Jesus Christ is Lord,
          to the glory of God the Father." Philippians 2:9-11
The lion will lie down with the lamb and peace will reign.
All hands, all voices will be raised in praise
  to you, Father,
  to you, Jesus, our Messiah,
  to you, Holy Spirit, our strength.
All men will praise you for who you are and what you have done.
  Your compassion never fails,
    your mercy and forgiveness have redeemed us from the pit,
      set our feet upon the path of righteousness.
  Who is man, that you should be mindful of him,
    you who created all things, past, present and future?
    We are but a fleeting mist in this place,
      but you have made for us an eternal home with you.
    How can we not praise you?
      How can our hearts not be filled with gratitude
        and rejoicing?
Let each man, each woman who reads or hears these words
  go forth and proclaim this message to a lost and dying world.
This day is a gift,
  the call to the cross of Calvary is a treasure,
    eternity in the light of Christ Jesus
      is a promise to be grasped and accepted,
        but another tomorrow in this place is not guaranteed.

Help us, O Lord, to live this day for you,
   to live this day as though there may be no tomorrow here,
      to live this day according to your plan and purpose
         for each one of us.
We love you Lord, for you have made a way
   when there seemed to be no way,
      you lifted us higher than our dreams,
         higher than our loudest "Hallelujah".
Go before us into this day and strengthen us,
   that we may not fail to bear the shield of faith
      and wield the sword of the Spirit, which is your Holy Word.
We love you.
   We are your redeemed.
   We are your children indeed.
                    Amen.

"Praise the Lord, O my soul, and forget not all his benefits—
who forgives all your sins and heals all your diseases,
who redeems your life from the pit and crowns you with love
and compassion, who satisfies your desires with good things
so that your youth is renewed like the eagle's."
Psalm 103:2-5

You Listen For My Call

My Father in heaven, hallowed be your name.
  Thank you my Father, for loving me,
    for holding me close and not turning from me.
  You do not abandon, you do not condemn.
  The day has promise,
    an inner peace exists because of you.
  I love you and thank you,
    for you have blessed me and my family greatly.
  Jesus, I look forward to a hug from you
    and a "Well done, good and faithful servant."
My heavenly Father, you are so good to me.
  I can come to you any time, night or day, and you hear me.
  You listen for my call,
    my voice is familiar to you and you are pleased to answer -
      to lift up, to give strength, and to build faith in me.
  Without you life would be a disheartening struggle
    with naught but the grave on the distant horizon.
  Without you there would be no hope for true redemption,
    no promise of life eternal in paradise.
  How can I, an unworthy sinner, saved only by your grace,
    praise you enough?
  Surely your mercy and love will follow me all the days of my life
    and the testimony of my lips
      will be of your ever-loving goodness and mercy.
  Go before me into this day and use me for your purposes,
    your glory and your good pleasure.
    Let the cry of the lost and the wounded be a call to action,
      a call to true discipleship.
        I love you.
            Amen.

"You are forgiving and good, O Lord, abounding in love to all
   who call to you.
Hear my prayer, O Lord; listen to my cry for mercy.
In the day of my trouble I will call to you,
   for you will answer me,"
                    Psalm 86:5-7

You Made A Way Eternal

My Father in heaven, hallowed be your name.
  The heavenly host sings praises to your name.
    "Hallelujah for He is mighty, He is just,
      He is loving, his compassion never ends.
      Praise the name of the Mighty One,
        for he has created all things seen and unseen,
          all things past, and all things yet to come."
Lord God, there is no world that you did not set into being,
  no child that you did not form in that secret place.
The sun rises and the sun sets because of you, O God.
  The day begins and the day ends according to your design.
Who is man that he should boast of his accomplishments,
  let him boast in you.
Who is man that he should take pride
  in his wisdom and knowledge,
    your thoughts are so much higher than his,
      your wisdom and knowledge are boundless and complete.
You are the Creator, we are the created.
You are eternal, we are but a fleeting mist in this earthly form.
Thank you, Lord God, that you have made a way eternal
  for those who seek your face,
    those who come to the throne on bended knee.
You have given a Way where there seemed to be no way,
                  Truth where there is no truth,
                    Life where all else leads to lasting death.
You are holy.
We give you praise, and honor, and glory.
Your compassion and forgiveness are beyond the mind of man.
Change us.
Cleanse and sanctify us with the mighty waters of the Holy Spirit.
Renew our minds in the power of your Word.

Let praise be ever in our hearts and on our lips
   for your faithfulness,
      your unconditional and unending love.
You are holy.
   Blessed be your name.
Amen.

> *"For God so loved the world that he gave his one and only Son, that whoever believes in him shall not perish but have eternal life. For God did not send his Son into the world to condemn the world, but to save the world through him."*
> *John 3:16-17*

You Place Gifts On The Path

My Father in heaven, hallowed be your name.
Thank you Lord God for today,
for the array of opportunities ahead to serve you.
Many are the joys that you place in my path.
Even in times of sorrow and hardship you place gifts on the path;
opportunities
to lift up the broken,
to provide for the needy,
to give hope to the lost.
Open the eyes of my heart to your will in all things great and small,
lest I stumble on the stones of comfort,
selfishness and disobedience.
Let the joy of my salvation be evident to all.
Let the words of my mouth be measured , reasoned,
and full of grace, that no boastful or unwholesome thing
would pass through my lips.
Today is a day that you have wrought,
in it there is true meaning and hope.
May the testimony of my yesterdays
and praise for the redeeming work of the risen Savior
be used to minister to the wounded,
to draw the despairing to the Light.
I can do no good and lasting thing without you,
no good and lasting thing without the power of the Spirit
and the truth of your Word.
I thank you and praise you my Father.
Amen

"Is not this the kind of fasting I have chosen;
to loose the chains of injustice and untie the cords of the yoke,
to set the oppressed free and break every yoke?
Is it not to share your food with the hungry and to provide the poor
wanderer with shelter —when you see the naked, to clothe him,
and not to turn away from your own flesh and blood?
Then your light will break forth like the dawn, and your healing
will quickly appear; then your righteousness will go before you,
and the glory of the Lord will be your rear guard.
Then you will call, and the Lord will answer;
you will cry for help, and he will say; 'Here am I.'."
Isaiah 58:6-9

You Raised Me Up

My Father in heaven, hallowed be your name.
Your kingdom come, your will be done, on earth as it is in heaven.
  Thank you Lord, for hope in you,
    for freedom and life in you.
  In this world of war and hatred there is no true peace except in you.
  Should tomorrow never come
    you have promised a forever tomorrow
      for all who have knelt at the foot of Calvary's tree
        and confessed that "Jesus is Lord",
       for all who have been lifted up by the sight of the empty tomb,
        for it is written:

> *"That if you confess with your mouth "Jesus is Lord",*
> *and believe in your heart that God raised him from the dead,*
> *you will be saved. For it is with your heart that you believe*
> *and are justified, and it is with your mouth that you confess*
> *and are saved." Romans 10:9-10*

Lord God, I could not save myself, but you made a way.
I could not see my sin, but you opened the eyes of my heart.
I was lost on the roads of darkness
  but your hand placed me on the lighted path.
I knew emptiness and despair,
  but you filled me and gave me hope.
I lived in a night of sorrow and complaint,
  but you drew me into the morning of joy and praise.
Let my lips always honor you
  and may I share the reason for the gladness of my heart
    with the lost,
      the discouraged,
      the oppressed,
        and those without hope.
Let me never forget that I was lost and now am found.
Let me always remember to give you all the praise and honor
  for who you are and all you have done.

Who is like you, o Lord,
   your compassion is boundless,
   your forgiveness beyond the mind of man,
   your love is never ending.
I love you my Father,
          Savior, Lord and friend,
          Counselor, Comforter and Strength.
You raised me up from the pit of defeat,
   you allowed me to soar on the wings of victory.
              Amen.

"O Lord my God, I called to you for help and you healed me.
O Lord, you brought me up from the grave;
  you spared me from going down into the pit.
Sing to the Lord, you saints of his; praise his holy name."
            Psalm 30:2-4

You Release The Captives

My Father in heaven, hallowed be your name.
  Thank you for rest, for peace, for joy.
  The day holds much in store because of you.
  You go before and behind me,
    your hand of grace and protection is upon me.
  You are my Father and I am your child.
    Teach me your precepts and help me to walk in your ways.
      Were I to turn to the right or to the left,
        should sinful desires of the flesh threaten to overtake me,
          convict me in the power of the Spirit and bring me back
            to the path of righteousness and victory.
My Who is like you, almighty God?
  Your forgiveness is beyond measure,
    your compassion is beyond all that the human heart can know,
    your power releases the captives
      from the prisons of woundedness, hopelessness and sin.
Who else can stand outside the tomb of death and decay
  and command the captive to come out?
My Lord, my God, you bring victory over defeat,
  hope over despair,
    and joy in the morning.
I praise you my Father,
          Savior, Lord and Friend,
          Counselor, Comforter and Strength.
            Amen.

"The Spirit of the Lord is upon me, because he has anointed me
   to preach good news to the poor.
He has sent me to proclaim freedom for the prisoners
   and recovery of sight for the blind, to release the oppressed,
   and proclaim the year of the Lord's favor."
              Luke 4:18-19

You Turned Away From Him For Me

My Father in heaven, hallowed be your name.
   Your kingdom come, your will be done, on earth as it is in heaven.
   You are so awesome, Lord God.
      You see all things, know all things, and created all things,
         yet you know each man, each woman, each child by name.
            You care about each one and you desire
               that no one should perish.
      You have given me, a sinner undeserving of your grace,
         forgiveness and true life in Christ Jesus.
      You heard the cry of my heart and the repentance from my lips
         and you lifted me from darkness.
      Who is like you, O Lord?
         Who else can love the vilest sinner with an unconditional love,
            a love expressed on Calvary's hill?
               You placed all of my sins upon your only son Christ Jesus
                  on that day.
               For those dark hours you turned away, forsook him,
                  for you could not look upon humanity's sin.
               Never before had you forsaken him,
                  and never again will you ever look away
                     from your beloved Son.
               You raised him up in glory and there is no other name
                  by which we must be saved.
   It is written in your most precious Word
      that you will never leave or forsake me,
         that you will raise me up on the last day.
   I thank you my Father, for all you have done
      and will ever do.
      My heart is full of gratitude and my spirit rejoices,
         for I was lost and now am found,
            was in darkness and now know the Light,
               was in despair but now know a joyous hope.

Who is greater than you, O Lord?
You go into the day before, behind and within me,
your blessed hope sustains me,
and I will dwell in the house of the Lord forever.
Amen.

"From the sixth hour until the ninth hour darkness came over all the land. About the ninth hour Jesus cried out in a loud voice, 'Eloi, Eloi, lama sabachthani?'—which means, 'My God, my God, why have you forsaken me?'"
Matthew 27:45-4

You Will Lift Up My Head

My Father in heaven, hallowed be your name.
  Father, you hear the cry of my soul,
    you know all that there is to know about me.
  Why is my head so downcast, O Lord?
    Surely the knowledge that your hand is upon me
      should lift me from the spirit of heaviness.
    Surely your Word of life
      should bring confidence and enthusiasm.
  Here, in the valley, you are with me,
    and I will yet celebrate your name
      and the assurance of my salvation.
  Who is like you, O Lord?
    You are my Father, I am your child.
      I find comfort and rest in your bosom.
      Your purpose for me is sure and eternal.
  You will lift up my head in due time
    and I will walk with quickened step
      on the path you have designed.
  I thank you and praise you, for my true life is in you.
    All things of this earthly life will come and go as the seasons,
        but I will stand on the solid rock that is Christ Jesus.
  You are the same yesterday, today and tomorrow.
    My hope is in you.
                    Amen.

> *"I am still confident of this:*
> *I will see the goodness of the Lord in the land of the living.*
> *Wait for the Lord; be strong and take heart and wait for the Lord."*
> *Psalm 27:13-14*

Your Love Is All I Need

My Father in heaven, hallowed be your name.
  You created all things great and small,
    you see all things, know all things,
      I am in awe of you.
My Savior and Friend, precious is your name.
  Your name is above all names,
    you are the Lamb that was slain,
      I am in awe of you.
I praise you and thank you my Father, and you my Savior,
  for you have not left me as an orphan.
      You have sent the Counselor, the Spirit of truth,
        to be with me and within me.
      It is through the Spirit that you are in me and I am in you.
  You love when I can not love,
    you see when I can not see,
    you hear when I do not hear,
    you speak when I can not speak,
    your compassion is boundless and never ending.
  When I fall you lift me up,
    when I am weak you gird me up,
    when I am tired you carry me,
    when I am discouraged you give me hope.
  There is great joy in my salvation,
    a quiet peace enfolds me during the battles of the day.
  Help me to listen to the whispers of the Holy Spirit.
  Steady my feet upon your path and draw me to the destiny
    that you have ordained.
  Search my heart and cast out all that is unlovely
    and without grace.
  O Lord, you are the great healer,
    place your hand upon my wounds
      and deliver me from the bondage of past hurts.
  You are my Father and I am your child.
    Incline your ear to me and bless me, that I may bless
      others.
    Fulfill your purposes in and through me for your glory.

I am your child and you are my Father.
Your love is all I need.
Amen.

"But I am like an olive tree flourishing in the house of God;
I trust in God's unfailing love for ever and ever.
I will praise you forever for what you have done;
in your name I will hope, for your name is good.
I will praise you in the presence of your saints."
Psalm 52:8-9

Your Promises

My Father in heaven, hallowed be your name.
  Your kingdom come, your will be done, on earth as it is in heaven.
  You are Lord and Master of all things great and small,
    yet you are my "Abba" Father, my "Daddy" Father.
  No man is without sin.
    No earthly father can love as you love -
      completely, unconditionally and eternally.
Abba, you knew me even while I was in my mother's womb.
  Your loving hand has been upon me all the days of my life.
    Even when I was steeped in ignorance, pridefulness
      and rebellion you were there.
    You did not turn from me, you saw my woundedness
      and did not abandon me to the pit.
    You have held my hand and walked with me
      in times of great sorrow and distress.
    Before I knew you your guardian angels watched over me
      and protected me, snatching me many times
        from the edge of the abyss.
My heavenly Dad, who is like you?
  I thank you and praise you for all that you are to me
    and all that I am to you.
      I am precious in your sight, O Lord,
        and I can scarcely take that in.
  You have opened the eyes and ears of my heart
    that I may hear the whispers of the Holy Spirit
      and see your eternal goodness.
  Your promises give me great peace, hope and joy.
    Were I to count all of my days the sum of them
      would be as a moment in eternity,
        a brief chapter in your eternal book of life.
Go before me into this day Abba Father,
  take my hand and lead me in your ways.
    Let the words of my mouth
      and the meditations of my heart be pleasing to you, O Lord.

I love you Abba Father,
I love you Jesus my Savior, Lord and Friend,
I love you Holy Spirit my Counselor, Comforter and Strength.
Amen.

"Praise the Lord.
Praise God in his sanctuary; praise him in his mighty heavens.
Praise him for his acts of power;
*   praise him for his surpassing greatness.*
Praise him with the sounding of the trumpet,
*   praise him with the harp and lyre,*
praise him with tambourine and dancing,
*   praise him with the strings and flute,*
praise him with the clash of cymbals,
*   praise him with resounding cymbals.*
Let everything that has breath praise the Lord.
Praise the Lord."   Psalm 150:1-6

A Conversation with My Heavenly Father

INTRODUCTION:

The following conversation was recorded in my prayer journal as it transpired over a number of weeks in our Sunday morning adult education program called "Experiencing The Father's Love". The program had the core objectives of helping us to listen and wait before the Lord, and to allow ourselves to simply be loved by him. During this precious time of individual quiet time and prayer the focus was the deepening of our relationship with our Heavenly Father. While this conversation was held between my heavenly Father and me, it is general in content and, I believe in varying ways and degrees it applies to all of us who have been called.

This conversation transpires over the next seven pages.

Conversation – Parts 1 & 2

1.

"The heavenly hosts sing over you, my child,
rejoice over you,
for you were once lost and now am found.
Your heart is for me my child,
and I am drawing you nearer.
Rest in me.
I am loving and gentle
and my touch is affirming and restoring.
Rest in me,
and you will rise up on the wings of the dawn
to the sounds of the angelic choir.
Is there any good thing
that I would withhold from you?
Your Abba Father."

2.

Yes, my Father,
the stars above me,
the earth below,
all that is seen and unseen,
all that is known and unknown,
is the work of your hands,
your thoughts.
All of this Father, is from you,
yet you know me,
your loving hand is upon me,
your compassion soothes and heals
the cares and wounds
of this, and other days.
Who is like you, my heavenly Dad,
you who draws me gently closer
that I may know you more,
that I may rest in the cradle of your arms.
I love you Abba Father, who is like you?

Conversation – Part 3

3.

"My child, I have seen your tears,
I have heard your laughter.
From the beginning I have been with you –
you did not see me, you seldom heard my voice,
but I have been with you, watching over you
as a mother hen watches over her chicks
and protects them.
The evil one has tried to discourage you,
to lead you away,
to wrench you from my loving hand,
but my grasp is firm and eternal.
Have I not lifted you
from the chasm of hopelessness
and placed you on a high place of joy?"
My child, rest in me.
Draw ever so close and know my compassion and love
in a new way, a way without bounds, a way without doubts,
a way of freedom and great joy.
I love you, my child,
you are my delight, my precious child forever.
Your Abba Father."

Conversation – Part 4

4.

Thank you Father, for your words of comfort and affection.
Thank you for reminding me that you are with me always,
that you are beside me in all seasons,
lifting me from the briars and the tares,
dancing with me in summer fields of joy.
You draw me closer, there are no wounds, no scars
that your love's light can not pierce and soften.
I began as a child and now you are changing me,
healing me, that I may be a child again.
O, the wonder of your nearness, your embrace;
no conditions I must meet.
Your child am I, loved without bounds,
learning to love without bounds.
Who is like you, my heavenly Dad,
You are my all in all.

Conversation – Part 5

5.

Thank you Father, for this day,
for each and every yesterday,
for each tomorrow you've ordained for me.
Lord, where sin remains, has hold,
open the eyes of my heart that I might see, repent, be free.
Where there is darkness
shine your light as in the dawn of day
bidding the shadows fade away.
"My child, have you given all to me?
Have you left the altar of all earthly things
and walked the holy way?
Have you heard the child cry
but focused on the noises of the day?
Have you seen the downcast man, the anguished mom,
and failed to speak of hope in me?
Have you sensed the Wind a-blowing
but turned and walked another way?"

Conversation -- Part 6

6.

Yes, My father you know the all of me,
when I rise up, when I lay down, when I go out, when I come in.
You know my deepest thoughts,
there's no well so deep your sight can not the bottom reach,
no faint echo to your ear is lost or indistinct.
My Lord your gentle admonition touches sure.
Forgive me, for I've not left all earthly, fleshly things,
nor always heard the children's cries,
lifted up the hurting man, the anguished mom,
embraced the Spirit's quiet breeze and moved in faith
in an unselfish and unhurried way.
Lord Jesus, shine your light before each step today,
let me walk with purpose, love, humility.
Who is like you O Lord, my Father, Savior, Lord and Friend,
my Counselor, Comforter and Strength.
I love you.
Let me love you more than life,
more than I could ever dream or say.

Conversation – Part 7

7.

"My child, from sunrise to sunset to sunrise
you are ever before me.
In times of laughter, in seasons of sorrow
I am so very close to you.
When storms come and savage winds threaten,
my steady, loving hand is upon you.
When, in the morning, peace and joy envelop you,
you will know it is my embrace.
See the seasons flow, the wondrous shades of greens
and autumn reds, oranges and gold.
Know that all the palettes touched by my brush
give colors uniquely for your eyes and heart.
Go, my child, into the seasons of this life with me,
holding my hand in true assurance,
in quiet anticipation of the glory of your distant home."

Conversation – Part 8

8.

Yes, my Father, I know the peace of your embrace.
You are drawing me ever closer with your healing hand,
dispelling fear's shadows with your light.
I love you, your compassion and caring is without bounds,
you are all-powerful, but your tenderness softens
the hardened corners of my heart,
it is a healing balm to my woundedness.
Thank you, Father, for the seasons I have seen,
the rainbows of joy that came after sorrow's rain.
Thank you for the colors of the seasons
made so wondrous for my eye and precious for my soul.
I've heard the sounds of children playing,
the words of forgiveness spoken and received.
You've given me birds' songs in the early morn,
the laughter of lovers at noon,
praise for you from angelic choirs
in the quiet evening of my mind.
Thank you Abba, for going before, behind and around me
into this day and into all the days you have purposed for me.
Who is like you, you lifted me from the pit
and gave me true life.

Conversation – Part 9

9.
Father God, I love you.
Jesus, my Savior, Lord and Friend. I love you.
Holy Spirit, my Counselor, Comforter and Strength, I love you.

"My child, let this day be lived for me.
Forget about yourself and be in me.
Let the Spirit reign in power in your heart and soul,
leading you on the path of healing, change and righteousness.
I have forgiven you your trespasses, now forgive yourself.
Let your yes be yes and no be no.
Lift up my name in prayer and praise,
for I am your all in all.
You are loved deeply and my plan for you is amazing.
Do not be fearful, for I am with you.
Know that my strong right hand goes before you
all the days of your life.
Trials will come and go,
blessings and laughter will abundantly flow,
and I will be with you always.
Your Abba Father."

AMEN.

Let us walk on the smooth stones
of gratitude and praise
that frequent the path
the Lord has set before us.

Jesus loves you
and so do I.

About The Author

Robert (Bob) Sexton lives in Lincoln, Rhode Island with his wife Ellie. He has four adult children and thirteen grandchildren. Before retirement in 1995, Bob enjoyed a successful career in the information processing field. He is active in his local Assembly of God Church and has served the church body as a lay-leader and volunteer in the areas of Christian Twelve Step Recovery Programs and adult education. He currently serves on the Finance Committee and the Church Council. Bob has been mightily blessed in recent years by participating in a number of missions projects in poor neighborhoods in San Martin and La Libertad, El Salvador.

Made in the USA
San Bernardino, CA
30 November 2014